THE
MĀSHÎAḤ

THE
מָשִׁיחַ

A Study of the Messianic Prophecies

THE LOVING-KINDNESS OF G-D | VOLUME TWO

MARK STOUFFER

ISBN: 979-8-9888291-6-4 (paperback)

ISBN: 979-8-9888291-4-0 (e-book)

ISBN: 979-8-9888291-5-7 (audiobook)

Note: in some cases, the verse numbers in the Tanakh are different from those in the Christian Bible. In this book, when such verses are cited, the verse numbers from the Tanakh are displayed in parentheses after the verse numbers from the Christian Bible.

Cover design and interior formatting by Rachael Ritchey

This past Saturday evening (1 December 2001), in a well-coordinated attack, two Palestinian suicide bombers detonated their charges in a crowded pedestrian mall in the heart of Jerusalem. At the time of the blast, the mall was packed with civilians, many of them teenagers and children, sitting at outdoor cafes and patronizing shops, restaurants and discos. Several minutes later, a car bomb exploded in a nearby alley. The third bomb was clearly intended to harm the medical workers and rescue personnel that had arrived on the scene to tend to the wounded. In total, 10 Israelis between the ages of 14 and 20 were killed and 180 were wounded, several of them seriously. . ..

Letter dated 4 December 2001 from the Permanent Representative of Israel (Yehuda Lancry) to the United Nations addressed to the Secretary-General

Fast forward 22 years to today:

On 7 October, Israel woke to the sound of rocket fire and ongoing sirens. Unfortunately, the sound of sirens is all too familiar to the Israeli ear, but the massacre that followed was an event the likes of which have not been seen since the Holocaust. This is not another round of fighting, not another operation, this is a war initiated by Hamas. The ISIS-like terror organization Hamas infiltrated Israel's borders while slaughtering the civilian population in their peaceful communities. Entire families were brutally murdered, children, mothers, fathers and grandparents were burned alive, tortured and executed by these barbaric Hamas terrorists with unparalleled savagery. Israeli women were raped and paraded through the streets of Gaza. . ..

Letter dated 6 November 2023 from the Permanent Representative of Israel (Gilad Erdan) to the United Nations addressed to the Secretary-General and the President of the Security Council

One day G-d will provide a solution to the problem of Gentile violence against His people. He will send the Messiah to deliver the Jews in the fullness of time. There is extensive prophecy about the Messiah and this event in the Tanakh.

CONTENTS

ACKNOWLEDGMENTS

I greatly appreciate all the help I have been given with this book!

Thank you, Amy Lyle, for doing the initial grammar check. Thank you, beta readers, Haven Barker, Stephanie D'Amico, Collin Marshall, Behzad Namazi, and Michael Tompkins. You did a great job.

Thank you, Howard Silverman, for the cultural check, and thank you, Jim Swearingen, for the final review. Thank you, Rachael Ritchey, for the great cover and formatting.

Thanks to J.R. Klein for helping with the pronunciation of the Hebrew words. In addition, thanks to Dennis Kambury for the excellent narration.

Thanks to the launch team for stepping forward to help me promote this book. Thank you, Joyce Aubuchon, Dave Baker, Julie Barker, Nancy Barker, Victoria Bonner, Carol Bradley, Carolyn Brubaker, Candice Coates, Dan Durkin, Tom Eisele, Kathy Friedberg, Todd Friedberg, Tim Gerwin, Ben Gibbons, Scott Herrmann, John Hoban, Karen Johnson, Reyne Kaiser, Amir Khodadoust, Tony Khoury, Lisa Kreitzer, Paul Kruggel, Sam Maxwell, Darlene McCallum, Greg Morgan, Andy Morris, Scott Neely, Charlotte Patin, Lara Phelps, Dave Powers, Dave Purvis, Diane Ritchie, Patrick Schumer, Dan Scott, Chuck Sheridan, Chip Shillington, Anna Sopher, Jami Staples, Dave Stouffer, Gilbert Stouffer, Lisa Thomas, Rich Thompson, Andy Watkinson, and Darlene Yost.

Thank you, Ramiz from Fiverr, for working so hard and making such a great website.

Thank you, Jenny Johnson, Jim Swearingen, Rich Thompson, and Oleg Vernikoff, for the great videos you made for the website. Thank you, Adam Anderson, for your assistance with my social media accounts and the videotaping.

Thanks to Stacey Chillemi, Henry Duodu, Deborah Henne, Dallas Monticue, Paul W. Reeves, and Robert Thibodeau for having me on your podcasts. I appreciate the opportunities you gave me to promote these books. I enjoyed the time I spent with each of you.

Thanks to my home church for your prayers.

Thank you, Noushi, for all of your assistance contacting people. More importantly, thank you for lovingly granting me an unlimited amount of time to work on these books.

Thank you, G-d, for your constant patience and grace. Thank you for all of the answered prayers. Thank you for the inspiration to write these books, and for giving me understanding into the Bible and ideas on what to write. Truth be told, these are actually Your books!

PREFACE

I am a Christian layperson. I have been studying and teaching the Bible for many years. I have read books written by both Jewish and Christian theologians. But more importantly, I have prayed that I might understand G-d's message in the Tanakh. Solomon wrote in Proverbs 2:4-5 that if you really want to know wisdom, and "if you seek her as silver, and search for her as for hidden treasure; then you will . . . discover the knowledge of G-d." I believe that G-d wants us to understand His message in the Tanakh, and I encourage you to pray to Him for understanding.

This is the second book in a four-volume series in which I am writing to Jewish laypeople. The goal of this series is to examine the Tanakh to see if it foretells Jesus, for He said that it does.

In the first book, we considered the element of sacrificial atonement in the Torah to see how well it foreshadowed Jesus' death on the cross. We also studied the lives of Isaac, Joseph, Moses, David, Daniel, and Cyrus, and we observed a number of similarities between their lives and Jesus' life. The question is, were these particular details from the lives of these heroes from the Tanakh recorded intentionally or coincidentally.

In this book, we will examine the messianic prophecies in the Tanakh, or Hebrew Bible, to see if they predict Jesus. For He claimed to be the Messiah. Of course, one of the main themes of Biblical prophecy is the coming of the Messiah. Admittedly, this subject is more difficult than the subject matter of Volume One. But studying it is well worth the effort. For the accuracy of the prophecies in the Hebrew Bible is extraordinary.

part four

PROPHECY

16

BIBLICAL PROPHECY

G-d can see the future.

In fact, He stands outside of time. We are not sure how that works, but we know that it does. For G-d has chosen to reveal select moments from the future to us. Some of the prophecies from the Hebrew Bible have already come to pass, and when they occurred, they took place exactly as G-d said they would. Indeed, G-d has placed prophecy in the Hebrew Bible so that we can find Him, for only He can see the future. But you have to care enough to take a look.

Over a period of a millennium, from the time of Moses up to the time of Malachi, G-d selected some of the Jews to be prophets. He gave them a vision, a dream, understanding, or even a quote regarding the future. There is actually quite a bit of prophecy in the Hebrew Bible.[1] Needless to say, every word

---

[1] 28% of the Hebrew Bible consists of the books of Isaiah, Jeremiah, and Ezekiel plus Daniel and the 12 minor prophets. There are also numerous other predictive prophecies throughout the

of it is of great importance. For, the events and people G-d chose to reveal in advance were picked because they convey a message about the human condition and His solution for our problems.

For those who are willing to read this prophecy, there are a number of aspects to be aware of that will help you understand its meaning:

1.   Prophecy Identifies G-d

One of the ways we can identify a true prophet versus a false prophet is that a real prophet is humble. They know they are just a regular human being and they have no special ability to see the future. It was G-d who showed it to them. In Daniel chapter 2, G-d gave King Nebuchadnezzar, the Babylonian king, a prophetic dream. But he had no idea what it meant. He wanted his wise men to interpret it for him, but he also wanted them to first declare, without being told, what his dream was. In this way, it would prove they knew what they were talking about and he would be able to trust their interpretation of the dream. Of course, no one could do that. However, G-d revealed to the Jewish captive, Daniel, the content of the dream and its interpretation. Daniel was brought before the king, and he said this:

> "As for the mystery about which the king has inquired, neither wise men, conjurers, magicians, *nor* diviners are able to declare *it* to the king. However, there is a G-d in heaven who reveals mysteries, and He has made known to King Nebuchadnezzar what will take place in the latter days. This was your

---

remainder of the Hebrew Bible starting in Genesis chapter 3 where God made a prediction to Eve.

dream and the visions in your mind while on your bed. As for you, O king, *while* on your bed your thoughts turned to what would take place in the future; and He who reveals mysteries has made known to you what will take place. But as for me, this mystery has not been revealed to me for any wisdom residing in me more than *in* any *other* living man, but for the purpose of making the interpretation known to the king, and that you may understand the thoughts of your mind."[2]

Then Daniel went on to reveal the dream and its interpretation. King Nebuchadnezzar was very impressed.[3] In this quote, we can see Daniel's humility. He knew, and he wanted everyone else to know, that it is G-d who sees the future.

Isaiah quotes G-d who makes the same point, only more forcefully. In Isaiah chapter 41, G-d draws a line in the sand and calls on the man-made gods of the ancient world to prophesy as He does:

"Declare the things that are going to come afterward, that we may know that you are gods; Indeed, do good or evil, that we may anxiously look about us and fear together. Behold, you are of no account, and your work amounts to nothing; he who chooses you is an abomination."[4]

---

[2] Dan. 2:27-31 (27-30).

[3] Dan. 2:46-48.

[4] Isa. 41:23-24.

Of course, they can't prophesy. Indeed, they were imagined and do not exist. But He does. Thus, He tells us that:

> ". . . I am G-d, and there is no one like Me, declaring the end from the beginning and from ancient times things which have not been done, saying 'My purpose will be established, and I will accomplish all My good pleasure'; . . ."[5]

There is astonishing prophecy in the Hebrew Bible including many compelling prophecies in the book of Isaiah itself. Many of these prophecies have already come to pass, and some pertain to the time of the end and still remain to be fulfilled. By studying prophesy in the Hebrew Bible, our faith is strengthened as we encounter hard evidence that the G-d of the Jews is the one true G-d.

2. Short-Term vs. Long-Term Predictions

G-d gave His prophets short-term prophecies as well as prophecies that would take place in the far distant future. In this way, each prophet could be validated by the people of his day. The penalty for being a false prophet was death.[6] Therefore, there was a strong incentive not to fake it. It was an important safety mechanism so that the Jewish people could know they were hearing G-d's words.

An example of a short-term prophecy is Isaiah's prophecy which he gave when the Assyrian army arrived outside of Jerusalem during the reign of the Assyrian king, Sennacherib. At this time, King Sennacherib and his army were strong and had been victorious over many nations. Sennacherib sent

---

[5] Isa. 46:9b-10.
[6] Deut. 18:15-22.

Rabshakeh as his spokesman.[7] Rabshakeh delivered a dire warning to the emissaries of King Hezekiah. He was convincing, and the Jews despaired.[8] However, Sennacherib erred in his arrogance as he spoke words of blasphemy against G-d. In the city, Hezekiah sent his key men to Isaiah to ask him to request G-d for protection against this blasphemer and his army. Isaiah responded to these men as follows:

> . . . "Thus you shall say to your master, 'Thus says the L-rd, "Do not be afraid because of the words that you have heard, with which the servants of the king of Assyria have blasphemed Me. Behold, I will put a spirit in him so that he shall hear a rumor and return to his own land. And I will make him fall by the sword in his own land.""[9]

Later, Isaiah sent an additional message to King Hezekiah:

> . . . "Therefore, thus says the L-rd concerning the king of Assyria, 'He shall not come to this city, or shoot an arrow there; neither shall he come before it with a shield, nor throw up a mound against it. By the way that he came, by the same he shall return, and he shall not come to this city,' declares the L-rd. 'For I will defend this city to save it for My own sake and for My servant David's sake.'"[10]

---

[7] Isa. 36:2; Hal Lindsey, *The Late Great Planet Earth* (New York, NY: Bantam Books, Inc., 1981) 13-14.

[8] Isa. 36:11 - 37:2.

[9] Isa. 37:6-7.

[10] Isa. 37:33-35.

Then it happened exactly as the L-rd said it would through Isaiah. For the angel of the L-rd went through the camp of the Assyrian army at night and struck 185,000 of the soldiers dead, just as the L-rd did to the firstborn of Egypt on the night of the first Passover. Sure enough, G-d revealed Himself yet again to the ancient world by protecting the Jews from a superior, hostile foreign power.[11] Furthermore, King Sennacherib did return home to his own land where he wound up being stabbed to death by two of his sons.[12]

Hence, the Jews of ancient Israel objectively knew they were hearing the words of G-d because of the accuracy of the short-term prophecies that He provided them through His prophets. But what about us today? We do not have the benefit of hearing a prophet at the present time, and nor have we seen the angel of L-rd strike the enemy's troops dead in the middle of the night.[13]

Not surprisingly, G-d has thought of us today as well. There may not be prophets today, but there are archaeologists. Isaiah prophesied approximately twenty-six and a half centuries ago. Many of Isaiah's long-term prophecies have already come to pass. Furthermore, many of Isaiah's prophecies were specific and verifiable. Christian Scholars who are liberal theologians try to find value in the Bible while denying that G-d has ever intervened miraculously in history. For example, they like to point out the good moral messages in the Bible. But they do not believe in prophecy.[14] However, so clear-cut are the prophecies in Isaiah that these scholars have been forced to come up with an explanation for

---

[11] Isa. 37:36.

[12] Isa. 37:37-38.

[13] Actually, the 6 Day War does bear a resemblance to the victory over the Assyrians.

[14] Gleason L. Archer, Jr. 336.

his prophecy other than what Isaiah claimed, that it came from G-d. Thus, they claim that Isaiah only wrote the first thirty-nine chapters, and that others wrote the remainder of the book later in history. For example, so detailed and accurate are the prophecies about the Jews' return from Babylonia that the liberal theologians have to postdate them, otherwise they would have to admit that these prophecies are real.[15] Liberal theologians cite differences in writing style and subject matter between the first thirty-nine chapters and the final twenty-seven to support their theory. But their foundational reason for breaking the book up into parts stems from their philosophical bias against the supernatural.[16]

Of course, G-d can see the future, and He was not surprised by the Age of Enlightenment and the development of liberal theology. Hence, in the same way that G-d saw to it that a copy of the Book of the Law was tucked away in the Temple for many years until it was found at just the right time;[17] so too, a series of important archaeological discoveries have been made in the modern age. These discoveries have verified the accuracy of the books of the Hebrew Bible, including their dates. For example, in 1947, an Arab shepherd boy happened upon a treasure trove of ancient scrolls of the Hebrew Bible.[18] The scrolls were stored in jars in a cave, and they were well preserved due to the arid desert climate. Thus, lo and behold, the very thing liberal scholars value - tangible evidence - was provided for them. Included in the scrolls was a complete copy of the book of Isaiah, dating from about

---

[15]   Isa. 44:28 - 45:7.

[16]   Gleason L. Archer p. 339.

[17]   2 Chron. 34:14-21.

[18]   Charles F. Pfeiffer, *The Dead Sea Scrolls and the Bible* (Grand Rapids, Michigan: Baker Book House, 1969) 13.

125 BCE.[19] Some of Isaiah's prophecies, like the prophecies about the return from Babylonia, came to pass before this date. But other prophecies came to pass after 125 BCE. For example, there are prophecies about Jesus' crucifixion in chapters 40 through 66 that took place about 150 years after the Isaiah Scroll was transcribed. Hence, modern archaeology has shredded the view that G-d did not give the ancient Jewish people actual prophecy. Therefore, we, like the Jews of antiquity who witnessed prophecies come true, can be confident in the authenticity of the prophecy in the Hebrew Bible.

3. Prophesy Has to Do with G-d's Plan in Human History and It Is Centered on the Jews

Biblical prophecy is not random. It is focused on the nation of Israel and the Messiah. Some of the prophecies have to do with Gentile nations or kings, but only insofar as they have significant dealings with the nation of Israel. Thus, there are prophecies regarding Cyrus, who would be a benefactor to Israel,[20] and Antiochus IV, who would act villainously towards the Jews.[21] Also, Daniel gives prophecies of the world empires that conquered Israel: Babylonia, Medo-Persia, Greece, and Rome. But there are no prophecies about The Buddha and the founding of Buddhism, Genghis Khan and the Mongols, the Middle Ages, the Renaissance, Napoleon, the rise of the United States, the Bolshevik Revolution in Russia, man setting foot on the moon, etc. For these leaders and events did not have any direct impact on the nation of Israel. As momentous and important as we may view these people and

---

[19] The Israel Museum, Jerusalem, "The dead Sea Scrolls\Explore the Dead Sea Scrolls-Online\Explore the Isaiah Scroll," n.d., http://dss.collections.imj.org.il/isaiah (accessed April 30, 2022).

[20] Isa. 44:26b - 45:6.

[21] Dan. 8:23-25.

events, they did not play a part in G-d's long-term plan to provide salvation to mankind.

In some cases, multiple prophets were given predictions regarding the same subject. For example, both Isaiah and Jeremiah prophesied about the impending downfall of Judah to the Babylonians. When there are multiple prophecies about a single subject, it tells us that G-d considers that event or person to be very important. Also, the different prophecies contain different details that fit together like a puzzle to give a more complete prediction of the event or person.

4. Prophecies Have Messages

Prophecies actually have two purposes. First, prophecies have been given to identify G-d; and second, there is a message in each prophecy. The messages given through the prophets to the Jewish people were often not very complimentary. They typically involved the need for the Jews to stop their wicked ways and turn back to G-d. Consequently, the prophets were hated. Some prophets wrote down their prophecies in books, and others gave their messages orally before the nation. Elijah was an oral prophet who Ahab and his pagan queen, Jezebel, detested. As it says in 1 Kings following Elijah's showdown with the prophets of Baal:

> Now Ahab told Jezebel all that Elijah had done, and how he had killed all the prophets with the sword. Then Jezebel sent a messenger to Elijah saying, "So may the gods do to me and even more, if I do not make your life as the life of one of them by tomorrow about this time." And he was afraid and arose and ran for his life and came to Beersheba, which belongs to Judah, and left his servant there. But he himself went a day's journey

into the wilderness, and came and sat down under a juniper tree; and he requested for himself that he might die, and said, "It is enough; now, O L-rd, take my life, for I am not better than my fathers."[22]

Indeed, it was not easy to be a prophet. Jezebel's sentiment towards Elijah is not atypical of the way the prophets were regarded. In Jeremiah's case, The L-rd spoke to him words of judgement for the nation. Then G-d said: "Perhaps the house of Judah will hear all the calamity which I plan to bring on them, in order that every man will turn from his evil way; then I will forgive their iniquity and their sin."[23] Jeremiah dictated the words of the L-rd to his scribe, Baruch. He then had Baruch read the scroll to the people in the Temple, for Jeremiah could not do that as he was restricted from entering the Temple. The people responded by fasting. When word of the scroll reached King Jehoiakim's ears, he ordered the scroll to be brought to him and read. Upon hearing a few columns from the scroll, Jehoiakim took it, cut it into pieces, and threw it in the fire. Then he called for Baruch and Jeremiah to be seized and brought into custody.[24]

Yet, even though the prophets were frequently disdained and mistreated by the Jewish kings and queens, they were honored by G-d. Upon sitting down under a juniper tree and praying for death, G-d sent an angel to comfort and encourage Elijah.[25] In the case of Jeremiah, G-d saw to it that he and Baruch were not found by the party sent by King Jehoiakim to arrest them. Instead, in much the same way that G-d inscribed a second set of stone tablets for Moses to take down the

---

[22] 1 Kin. 19:1-5.
[23] Jer. 36:3.
[24] Jer. 36:20-26.
[25] 1 Kin. 19:6-8.

mountain,[26] G-d oversaw Jeremiah dictating a new scroll to Baruch.[27]

In addition to the very real threats that were made against their lives, the prophets also had to cope with the revelation they received of the impending doom that lay in store in the future for the nation of Israel. These men had great hearts for G-d, and they loved the Jewish nation. They loved the mission G-d had for the Jews as His lone representatives amongst all the peoples of earth. But they also saw the sins of their fellow Jews. They understood why Israel would be judged, and it crushed them.[28] Perhaps they felt like those who lost fortunes in the stock market crash of 1929. Of course, those people only lost money. Many of the Jewish people squandered something far more priceless. Those who did not listen to the prophets lost the opportunity to be used by G-d to play a part in His mission.

In Daniel's case, the visions he saw of the future were so shocking that he became ill.[29] After seeing one vision, he was so troubled by what he saw that he prayed for more understanding. G-d sent a messenger who came to him. Their meeting was recorded in Daniel chapter 10:

> ". . . I lifted my eyes and looked, and behold, there was a certain man dressed in linen, whose waist was girded with a *belt of* pure gold of Uphaz. His body also was like beryl, his face had the appearance of lightning, his eyes were like flaming torches, his arms and

---

[26] Ex. 34:1.

[27] Jer. 36:27-32.

[28] Isa. 22:1-4; Jer. 20:14-18; Arthur Blech, The Causes of Anti-Semitism, A Critique of the Bible, rev. ed., (Amherst, NY, Prometheus Books, 2006), 279.

[29] Dan. 8:27.

feet like the gleam of polished bronze, and the sound of his words like the sound of tumult. Now I, Daniel, alone saw the vision, while the men who were with me did not see the vision; nevertheless, a great dread fell on them, and they ran away to hide themselves. So I was left alone and saw this great vision; yet no strength was left in me, for my natural color turned to a deathly pallor, and I retained no strength. But I heard the sound of his words; and as soon as I heard the sound of his words, I fell into a deep sleep on my face, with my face to the ground.

Then behold, a hand touched me and set me trembling on my hands and knees. And he said to me, "O Daniel, man of high esteem, understand the words that I am about to tell you and stand upright, for I have now been sent to you." And when he had spoken this word to me, I stood up trembling. Then he said to me, "Do not be afraid, Daniel, for from the first day that you set your heart on understanding *this* and on humbling yourself before your G-d, your words were heard, and I have come in response to your words."[30]

In this passage we get a glimpse of what it was like for a Jewish prophet to receive a vision. It was disturbing, and yet it was also a deep honor from G-d. A key sentence in this passage is the one that says that Daniel humbled himself and requested understanding. Daniel was exceptionally godly, and G-d obliged him. But the truth is that G-d wants to provide all

[30] Dan. 10:5-12.

of us with understanding, if we will only humble ourselves. It may not be as dramatic as Daniel's encounter with the man dressed in linen, but G-d is capable of using the message in the Hebrew Bible as well as speaking directly to our hearts to give us spiritual understanding.[31]

5. Common Mistakes in Prophetic Interpretation

A couple cautions about interpreting prophecy are: not to not spiritualize the meaning of a passage, and not to be dogmatic about prophecies that pertain to the future as of today. There are two predominant methods of interpreting prophecy: the "grammatical-historical," literal method, and the "spiritualizing" method.[32] In the first method, you interpret prophecy the same way you do the rest of scripture. You understand it per its face value meaning. Only if the language is figurative, or if the literal interpretation of a prophecy causes it to disagree with other prophecies or passages in the Bible, would you consider giving the prophecy a symbolic meaning.[33] In the spiritualizing method of interpretation, you are free to assign any meaning to a prophecy in order to make it fit with your overall prophetic and theological understanding of the Bible.[34] Certainly, prophecy does contain much symbology, but this is not a license for approaching it with the spiritualizing method of interpretation. It is often quite possible, based on the context of the passage, to understand G-d's intended meaning. Furthermore, sometimes the prophets even define their

---

[31] 1 Tim. 2:4.

[32] John F. Walvoord, *The Millennial Kingdom* (Grand Rapids, Michigan: Zondervan Publishing House, 1959) 59.

[33] Ibid., pp. 65-66.

[34] Ibid., pp. 59-66.

symbols in the text.[35] On the other hand, readers who approach a piece of prophecy seeking to find an interpretation that matches their beliefs will almost always find a reason why the prophecy agrees with their way of thinking. But rarely will they find the actual meaning of the prophecy.

One of the reasons why we do not understand the things of G-d very well is that we are so very different from Him. We see things differently than He does, and we may even project onto Him our human moral failings. We just cannot fathom how good and trustworthy He is. Therefore, we must set aside our biases and keep an open mind in order to be able to understand what He is trying to say to us. Furthermore, we need to read the Hebrew Bible using the grammatical-historical method of interpretation unless it is clear that the prophetic author is speaking figuratively. This is the way to hear G-d's message in the prophecy of the Hebrew Bible.

Today we can look back and see how the prophecies that have already taken place were fulfilled literally. However, pre-fulfillment, these prophecies did not always make sense, at least not from a human perspective. Therefore, we can expect prophecies that are not yet fulfilled to also take place literally. For example, we can see how this plays out in the story of the Abrahamic Covenant. The Abrahamic Covenant was not specifically a prophecy, but it did pertain to the future. In it, G-d made some promises to Abraham. Namely, He promised Abraham a vast number of descendants, a homeland for his descendants, and that through Abraham, all the families of the earth would be blessed.[36] This is clear enough, and yet when

---

[35] For example, in Daniel 8:21, after writing a prophecy featuring an aggressive shaggy goat, Daniel tells us that the goat represents a future Greek Empire that would supplant the Persian Empire.

[36] Gen. 12:1-3; 15:1-21; John F. Walvoord, *The Millennial Kingdom* 147-148.

no baby was forthcoming between Abraham and his wife, Sarah, they became confused. For Abraham and Sarah were human beings, and they were not patient in the way that G-d is. It is also the case that Abraham and Sarah were getting quite old. Therefore, from their perspective, G-d's promise must have meant something different than the plain meaning of the two of them having a baby. So, Sarah figured that maybe Abraham should try to have a baby with her maidservant, Hagar. Sure enough, the plan worked, and Hagar became pregnant. The problem was that their plan was not G-d's plan, and frankly, it was not a very good plan. In fact, Abraham caused a great deal of trouble by violating the sanctity of his marriage. But the point is that G-d's promise was literally fulfilled through Abraham and Sarah having a child, when the time was right according to G-d's plan. So too with prophecy, we can expect the prophecy about the end of time to take place the way it is predicted, even if we do not fully understand it. The question is not so much, what is going to happen, but rather, when is it going to happen.

Yet, we should not be overly certain of our interpretations of prophecies that still lie in the future. For the prophecies do not contain every detail about an event such that we can be dogmatic about their interpretations beforehand. Rather, the prophecies in the Hebrew Bible have differing levels of clarity. Some of them are hard to predict with any degree of certainty or specificity. But once they happen, then they come into focus such that we can see what the prophecies were predicting. In addition, we may also be able to see why G-d made some prophecies clear beforehand, but not others. G-d has a plan for humanity, and He is carrying it out in conformity with His attributes of patience, lovingkindness, faithfulness to His promises, justice, and moral perfection or righteousness. He has enemies, both earthly and heavenly. Therefore, He is strategic, and He has a timing for when to reveal truth and understanding. Hence, in some cases the prophecies are purposely vague until the moment when the event takes place. It is like a card game where you do not reveal your cards until just the right moment. Only it is not a game.

6. The Law of Double Reference

One of the mechanisms of Biblical prophecy which acts as a partial covering to conceal the timing of different future events is called the law of double reference. According to the law of double reference, the prophet is shown multiple events, but he combines them in the same prophecy. The events contain similar key elements, but they will take place in different eras. Thus, the prophecy may leave the reader with the misperception that it refers to a single event. An astute reader may sense that something is missing and have a feeling of uncertainty in terms of the outcome of the prediction. So initially, G-d is concealing that there are multiple events with time gaps between them. But once history has moved on and all of the events have taken place, then the prophecy becomes clear. In fact, then we gain a deeper understanding into the intrinsic meaning of the events as we see how there is a relationship between them.

A good example is the statement Jesus made in Luke chapter 4:

> And He came to Nazareth, where He had been brought up; and as was His custom, He entered the synagogue on the Sabbath, and stood up to read. And the book of the prophet Isaiah was handed to Him. And He opened the book, and found the place where it is written, "THE SPIRIT OF THE L-RD IS UPON ME, BECAUSE HE ANOINTED ME TO PREACH THE GOSPEL TO THE POOR.

> HE HAS SENT ME TO PROCLAIM
> RELEASE TO THE CAPTIVES, AND
> RECOVERY OF SIGHT TO THE BLIND,
> TO SET FREE THOSE WHO ARE
> DOWNTRODDEN, TO PROCLAIM THE
> FAVORABLE YEAR OF THE L-RD." And He
> closed the book and gave it back to the
> attendant, and sat down; and the eyes of all
> in the synagogue were fixed upon Him. And
> He began to say to them, "Today this
> Scripture has been fulfilled in your
> hearing."[37]

Here Jesus quoted Isaiah 61:1-2a. However, this is only part of the prophecy given in Isaiah 61. In fact, Jesus actually stopped in the middle of a sentence. Reading on starting in Isa. 61:2b, it says:

> ". . . and the day of vengeance of our G-d; to
> comfort all who mourn, to grant those who
> mourn *in* Zion, giving them a garland instead
> of ashes, the oil of gladness instead of
> mourning, the mantle of praise instead of a
> spirt of fainting. So they will be called oaks of
> righteousness, the planting of the L-rd that
> He may be glorified. . . ."[38]

Thus, here we see the second part of the prophecy consisting of the day of vengeance of G-d followed by the restoration of the beleaguered nation by the Messiah. The first part of the prophecy entailed the Messiah showing up and bringing good news to the downtrodden, the poor, the blind,

---

[37] Lk. 4:16-21.
[38] Isa. 61:2b-3.

and those who are in prison. In addition, the Messiah was also called to "proclaim the favorable year of the L-rd." Surely, this is a synopsis of what Jesus did two thousand years ago. He healed the blind and the sick, and He brought a message of G-d's love and forgiveness.

What no one saw is that there are actually two comings of the Messiah. The first one was two thousand years ago when Jesus accomplished the first part of His mission. The second one will be at the end of the time when He will return to put an end to the wicked governments of man and redeem Israel.[39] As He read this passage, Jesus was claiming to be the one predicted, and He was revealing that He would fulfill the prophecy in two stages. Of course, the overwhelming majority of Jewish people reject this interpretation of Isaiah 61, but the day will come and time will tell whether Jesus was right or not.

An example in the Hebrew Bible of a double-reference prophecy in which the time gap is not so hidden is Dan. 9:24-27. Coincidentally, it is related to the prophecy in Isaiah 61. This is a very important passage that we will study in depth in two other chapters, one in this book and the other in Volume 3.

* * * * *

Interestingly, the prophecies in the Christian New Testament fit together like a puzzle with the prophecies in the Hebrew Bible. New Testament prophecy does not cover any of the great leaders or developments in Gentile history either. It covers the future of Israel and the Messiah. New Testament prophecy mainly deals with the timeframe of the end of history. Part of Nebuchadnezzar's dream dealt with the "latter days." Indeed, there is much prophecy in the book of Daniel

---

[39] Dan. 2:35, 44.

dealing with the "end of the age"[40] or the "end time."[41] The Christian New Testament fits together with the book of Daniel regarding the tumultuous final seven-year period of history. The book of Revelation adds many details to the bare-bones outline of this period given in Daniel 9:26-27. Jesus also gave multiple details regarding the final period and the days leading up to it in His famous Olivet Discourse.[42] The final period will be the most horrendous time of suffering and war the world has ever known. This will be the case in Israel as well in the Gentile world. Speaking about Israel, Daniel wrote: "And there will be a time of distress such as never occurred since there was a nation until that time; . . ."[43] Speaking on the same subject, Jesus warned the Jews who will be alive at the end of time to flee Israel. He said: "But pray that your flight may not be in the winter, or on a Sabbath; for there will be a great tribulation such as has not occurred since the beginning of the world until now, nor ever shall."[44]

Thus, the prophecy in the New Testament covers the same subject matter as the prophecy in the Hebrew Bible. It just adds new details. The prophecy of the New Testament is also of a similar nature, writing style, and quality as that of the Hebrew Bible. It contains similar symbols, is specific as opposed to merely general, and is accurate based on the short-term prophecies that were given by Jesus regarding the events of 70 CE.

---

[40] Dan. 12:13.
[41] Dan. 11:35, 40; 12:4, 9.
[42] Mt. 24:1 - 25:46; Mk. 13:1-37; Lk. 21:5-36.
[43] Dan. 12:1.
[44] Mt. 24:20-21.

17

THE BIRTH OF THE MESSIAH

As babies are born in hospitals today, it is common for the new fathers to experience a particular set of emotions. It will be a unique combination they have never experienced before. They will be on "cloud nine," and they will feel true joy. They will feel relief that their new baby is healthy. They will have hope that their child will grow up to be happy and successful. They will be proud of their wives. Lastly, either in their mind or in their subconscious, they will feel like it was a miracle from G-d that their wife just gave birth to their child. And they will be right. Every baby and each of us are all miracles. Each of our lives is a precious gift from G-d.

However, some miracles are more miraculous. When Sarah gave birth to Isaac, it was a more spectacular miracle than other births. The reason is not because it was any harder for G-d, but because Sarah was barren. Of course, some women cannot have babies, or maybe it is a deficiency in their husband's body that prevents them from being able to get pregnant. In Sarah's case, we know she was barren as Abraham had already foolishly learned that he was capable of fathering a child. She was barren her whole life, and now she was very old. But then it happened. She conceived and gave birth to Isaac at the age of 90. It was a miracle.

G-d had told Abraham:

> ". . . I will make you a great nation, and I will bless you, and make your name great; and so you shall be a blessing; and I will bless those who bless you, and the one who curses you I will curse. And in you all the families of the earth shall be blessed."45

G-d had promised a son - and eventually a nation of descendants - many years before to Abraham and Sarah. Finally, Isaac came! This miracle birth got everyone's attention, but it was what G-d wanted to do through Abraham and Sarah's descendants that was most important. G-d had a plan to use this people to reach every family on earth and bless them. He did not share any more details of His plan at that point. But certainly, G-d was giving an indication of something that was going to happen that would be magnificent.

Furthermore, could it be that just as G-d's plan started with this special birth, one day there would be another special birth of an individual with a unique role from G-d?

Then G-d reinforced that He was going to do something magnificent for the sake of the world through the descendants of Abraham and Sarah when their daughter-in-law wound up being barren as well. So again, G-d intervened and healed

---

45 Gen. 12:2-3.

Rebekah's womb so that the line of descendants could go forward.[46]

Hence, Abraham and Sarah started a family. But soon thereafter, twists and turns started to appear in the family tree. Rebekah had twins. One of them was interested in the things of G-d, and one of them was not. He was Esau, and his line was not included in the family tree. They became a Gentile nation, the Edomites. Esau's brother, Jacob, had twelve sons and from them sprang the twelve tribes of Israel. Thus, Abraham, Isaac, and Jacob were the fathers of what would become the people of G-d. In addition, it was foretold that from the Jewish line would come a special person one day. G-d promised a people and a person. Certainly, there have been many important, godly Jews down through the ages. Men like Moses, Aaron, Joshua, Samuel, David, Solomon, Elijah, Daniel, and many others have led the nation to follow G-d. But greater than even them, it was prophesied that one day there would come a special one who would change everything. At the end of his life, Jacob spoke prophetic words to each of his sons about the tribes that would come forth from their families. When he came to Judah, he said this:

> "Judah, your brothers shall praise you; your hands shall be on the neck of your enemies; your father's sons shall bow down to you. Judah is a lion's whelp; from the prey, my son, you have gone up. He couches, he lies down as a lion, and as a lion, who dares rouse him up? The scepter shall not depart from Judah, nor the ruler's staff from between his

---

[46] Gen. 25:21.

> feet, until Shiloh comes, and to him shall be
> the obedience of the peoples. . ."[47]

This prophecy makes sense. Judah understood it, and so did his brothers. They were probably jealous. At some point in the future, Israel would become a nation, and once they did, it would be Judah's descendants who would be the kings. But then Jacob added another prophetic detail, and it was a little cryptic. He said that one day a special one would come from the line of Judah, and he would not just rule the Jewish people, but rather, he would command the obedience of all the peoples. The word Shiloh is not a name or a title. It is simply the Hebrew word šîlōh, and it means "whose it is."[48] In other words, G-d was prophesying about a very special person, but He was not revealing the identity of this person. Needless to say, G-d had a reason for not revealing that information at that time, and therefore, the Jewish people would have to wait until later to find out who this person is.

Sure enough, Jacob was right. That may seem amazing, but it is really not. For G-d can see the future, and G-d gave Jacob this piece of prophecy. Furthermore, G-d had a plan, and Judah was His choice to be the son of Jacob from whom would come the kings of the Jewish nation. Fast forward several hundred years to roughly 1000 BCE, and along came David, from the line of Judah. He became king when another man, from the tribe of Benjamin, who was not really interested in the things of G-d, was dismissed by G-d. But David treasured the things of G-d. Therefore G-d made a promise to him that from that point forward, the kings would

---

[47] Gen. 49:8-10.
[48] Walvoord and Zuck, eds., The Bible Knowledge Commentary, Old Testament Edition 98.

all come through his line, and so they did. Here are the words of G-d that were spoken to David through the prophet Nathan:

> "Now therefore, thus you shall say to My servant David, 'Thus says the L-rd of hosts, "I took you from the pasture, from following the sheep, that you should be ruler over My people Israel. And I have been with you wherever you have gone and have cut off all your enemies from before you; and I will make you a great name, like the names of the great men who are on the earth. I will also appoint a place for My people Israel and will plant them, that they may live in their own place and not be disturbed again, nor will the wicked afflict them any more as formerly, even from the day that I commanded judges to be over My people Israel; and I will give you rest from all your enemies. The L-rd also declares to you that the L-rd will make a house for you. When your days are complete and you lie down with your fathers, I will raise up your descendant after you, who will come forth from you, and I will establish his kingdom. He shall build a house for My name, and I will establish the throne of his kingdom forever. I will be a father to him and he will be a son to Me; when he commits iniquity, I will correct him with the rod of men and the strokes of the sons of men, but My lovingkindness shall not depart from him, as I took *it* away from Saul, whom I removed before you. And your house and your

kingdom shall endure before Me forever;
your throne shall be established forever."[49]

What an amazing prophecy, albeit the descendant of David's mentioned in this prophecy is not the future special king. Just before this beautiful pledge from G-d was spoken to David, David had told Nathan that he wanted to build G-d a permanent Temple because G-d still resided in the tabernacle. G-d replied to David: 'No, but rather I will build you a house.' But G-d meant something far greater than a dwelling. G-d meant that all the kings of Israel would now be descendants of David. The specific descendant mentioned in this prophecy is the very next king, David's son Solomon. G-d was telling David that Solomon would be given the privilege of building the Temple as opposed to him. Furthermore, G-d declared that the kingly line would proceed through Solomon, despite the fact that Solomon would commit sin.

All of the following kings were from the dynasties of David and Solomon. However, the kings that would issue forth from this line did not follow David's example as they typically did not have much of a heart for G-d. They wound up succumbing to arrogance as well as to a number of other sins. Nonetheless, G-d had made a promise, and G-d is faithful. The very next king after Solomon was his son, Rehoboam. He was young and arrogant. He was not godly like his grandfather or wise like his father. In fact, he was so off-putting that the country could not stomach him. It was at this point in time that Israel split in two, and there was a northern kingdom and a southern kingdom. Rehoboam retained the kingship of the southern kingdom, Judah, with Jerusalem as its capital.

This promise G-d made to David, also known as "the Davidic Covenant," was well known down through the ages in

---

[49] 2 Sam. 7:8-16.

Judah. The promise of a special king who would one day come also continued to be remembered. Hundreds of years after David, the prophets would foretell the special king to come, and they would call him "the Branch of David" or just "the Branch". For example, Isaiah, Jeremiah, and Zechariah all utilize these names in their prophecies about this person. Here is a passage from Jeremiah:

> "Behold, *the* days are coming," declares the L-rd, "when I shall raise up for David a righteous Branch; and He will reign as king and act wisely and do justice and righteousness in the land. In His days Judah will be saved, and Israel will dwell securely; and this is His name by which He will be called, 'the L-rd our righteousness.' . . ."[50]

Certainly, this is the special one promised from long ago, and He will come from the line of David. As king, He will be "righteous," "do justice and righteousness," and be called "the L-rd our righteousness." This is very striking. The Hebrew Bible is a large book. In places, it is a very symbolic book. But nowhere in the Bible is language like this used to describe a human being, king or not. In fact, the Hebrew word for L-rd in this passage is the name of G-d, YHWH.[51]

Here is another striking passage about this person:

> For a child will be born to us, a son will be given to us; and the government will rest on His shoulders; and His name will be called Wonderful Counselor, Mighty G-d, Eternal Father, Prince of Peace. There will be no end

---

[50] Jer. 23:5-6.
[51] Eiten Bar 101.

> to the increase of *His* government or of peace,
> on the throne of David and over his kingdom,
> to establish it and to uphold it with justice
> and righteousness from then on and
> forevermore. The zeal of the L-rd of hosts will
> accomplish this.[52]

This prophecy is well known. It is from Isaiah chapter 9, and it is poetic and beautiful. It is also clearly written, and yet, how can this be? How can this special person be recognized as "Mighty G-d" and also be born as a son to the Jewish people through the line of David? One thing is for sure, not David nor any of the kings that followed in his dynasty ever qualified to receive such praise. Most of the kings in his line were sinful. Although, every now and then, a godly king would come along. But they were guilty of misdeeds too, as they were human beings, and the Hebrew Bible was faithful to record their imperfections as well as their good qualities. For example, Hezekiah was a godly king who prayed to G-d and placed his faith in Him when the Assyrian army showed up and threatened Jerusalem.[53] Yet, the Hebrew Bible also reveals the distasteful level of selfishness that was in his heart.[54] In addition, neither he nor any other human king ever ruled over the whole world and established a state of righteousness and peace forevermore. Nonetheless, Hezekiah did place his faith in G-d, which is what G-d is looking for from all of us.

Here is another passage predicting the special one:

> Then a shoot will spring from the stem of
> Jesse, and a branch from his roots will bear
> fruit. And the Spirit of the L-rd will rest

---

[52] Isa. 9:6-7 (5-6).
[53] Isa. 36:22 - 37:20.
[54] Isa. 38 and 39.

on Him, the spirit of wisdom and understanding, the spirit of counsel and strength, the spirit of knowledge and the fear of the L-rd. And He will delight in the fear of the L-rd, and He will not judge by what his eyes see, nor make a decision by what His ears hear; but with righteousness He will judge the poor, and decide with fairness for the afflicted of the earth; and He will strike the earth with the rod of His mouth, and with the breath of His lips He will slay the wicked. Also righteousness will be the belt about His loins, and faithfulness the belt about His waist.[55]

In this word picture, we see the stump of a tree that has been cut down in which a shoot has sprung out, portending the potential regrowth of the tree. The stump is said to be David's father, Jesse. Many features line up between this passage and the passage in Jeremiah. Indeed, this is a prophecy about the same special person. He will be like G-d — righteous and faithful; and He will rule the earth with perfect justice.

But why does Isaiah not simply use the imagery of a branch growing out of a tree? Why does he use the image of a shoot coming from the stump of a fallen tree in this passage? Of course, a few thousand years have elapsed since Isaiah wrote these words, and now we know why. It is because eventually there came a day when the kings following Rehoboam were so bad for so long that G-d could no longer stomach them, and He put a stop to the dynasty. It happened in the time of Jeremiah, during the reign of King Jehoiakim.

---

[55] Isa. 11:1-5.

This repugnant king pushed G-d too far and everything spun out of control. G-d had given Jeremiah a prophecy for the Jewish people that was a warning. Out of His grace, G-d was giving them a chance to turn from their evil ways and stave off the judgement they deserved.[56] Jeremiah dictated the words of this prophecy to his scribe, Baruch, who wrote them down on a scroll.[57] When the scroll was brought to the king, he spurned it:

> Now the king was sitting in the winter house in the ninth month, with a *fire* burning in the brazier before him. And it came about, when Jehudi had read three or four columns, *the king* cut it with a scribe's knife and threw it into the fire that was in the brazier, until all the scroll was consumed in the fire that was in the brazier.[58]

That was how much King Jehoiakim thought of G-d's warning, and indeed, of G-d Himself. At that point, G-d could no longer go on with this king or even with this dynasty. Therefore, He brought judgement down upon King Jehoiakim:

> Then the word of the L-rd came to Jeremiah after the king had burned the scroll and the words which Baruch had written at the dictation of Jeremiah, saying, "Take again another scroll and write on it all the former words that were on the first scroll which Jehoiakim the king of Judah burned. And concerning Jehoiakim king of Judah you

---

[56] Jer. 36:3.
[57] Jer. 36:4.
[58] Jer. 36:22-23.

shall say, 'Thus says the L-rd, "You have burned this scroll, saying, 'Why have you written on it that the king of Babylon shall certainly come and destroy this land, and shall make man and beast to cease from it?' " Therefore thus says the L-rd concerning Jehoiakim king of Judah, "He shall have no one to sit on the throne of David, and his dead body shall be cast out to the heat of the day and the frost of the night. I shall also punish him and his descendants and his servants for their iniquity, and I shall bring on them and the inhabitants of Jerusalem and the men of Judah all the calamity that I have declared to them—but they did not listen." "[59]

Surely, Jehoiakim's corpse wound up being relegated to this ignominious fate. But what is really important is what happened to his line in the dynasty: G-d ended it. Certainly, G-d had to do it, but this new proclamation appeared to negate His promises to David and Solomon. The kingly line had followed a path for over four hundred years, and now G-d put a stop to it.

This is why Isaiah prophesied in chapter 11 that the special one would arise from the stump of Jesse. It is because G-d knew that at a point in time, the tree would be cut down. Yet, G-d could still bring forth a descendant from the family tree in the fulness of time to be the Messiah. Isaiah prophesied that this person would be like G-d, for He would be righteous and faithful. Yet, He would also be human for He would be a descendant of King David.

---

[59] Jer. 36:27-31.

Now let's look at the genealogy of Jesus. His lineages on His mother's side and his adoptive father's side are both given in the Christian New Testament. It turns out that Mary is a descendant of David, but not through Solomon. Rather, she is a descendant through another one of David's sons, Nathan.[60] Joseph, on the other hand, is a descendant of Jehoiakim and therefore, Solomon as well.[61]

When he comes to Joseph in Jesus' lineage, Matthew breaks his rhythm in which he had been repeating "to __ was born __," and instead he writes, "to Jacob was born Joseph the husband of Mary, by whom was born Jesus, who is called Christ."[62] In this way, Matthew is indicating that Joseph was not the actual father of Jesus, though Mary was His mother.

Thus, in a very unique way, Jesus' genealogy satisfies the conundrum created by G-d's rejection of Jehoiakim. G-d's promise to Solomon was, "I will establish the throne of his kingdom forever."[63] What is important to note in this sentence is that G-d did not make any promises to Solomon in regard to his descendants, only his throne. Hence, Jesus, who was the legal heir of Joseph as he was an adoptive son of Joseph, qualifies to sit on the throne of Solomon since Joseph was a descendant of Solomon. But Jesus was not a blood descendant of Solomon, thereby fulfilling G-d's pronouncement of judgment upon Jehoiakim.

On the other hand, Jesus was a blood descendant of King David through his mother, Mary. This is why the promised, special one is referred to as the Branch of David but never as the Branch of Solomon. For G-d promised to David that not only his throne, but also his descendants would endure

---

[60] Lk. 3:31.
[61] Mt. 1:6-16.
[62] Mt. 1:16.
[63] 2 Sam 7:13b.

forever.⁶⁴ Thus, quite stunningly, Jesus' lineage fulfills the promises G-d made to both David and Solomon despite the seeming dissolution of G-d's promises brought about by the faithless act of King Jehoiakim.

There is much prophecy in the Hebrew Bible predicting this special individual. It is interesting that included in this prophecy is the detail that this person would be born. This is an unusual detail for a prophecy. For example, in Isaiah, the prophecies about King Cyrus do not mention that one day he would be born. Of course he would be born. Everyone is born. Undoubtedly, astute readers of these prophecies noticed that the special one's birth was being predicted and wondered why. Surely there had to be something exceptional about this person's birth; otherwise, why would the prophets mention it?

After close to five and a half centuries following the return from Babylonia, Jesus' day came. In The Gospel According to Luke, we read that His birth was anything but normal:

> Now in the sixth month the angel Gabriel was sent from G-d to a city in Galilee, called Nazareth, to a virgin engaged to a man whose name was Joseph, of the descendants of David; and the virgin's name was Mary. And coming in, he said to her, "Hail, favored one! The L-rd is with you." But she was troubled at *this* statement, and kept pondering what kind of salutation this might be. And the angel said to her, "Do not be afraid, Mary; for you have found favor with G-d. And behold, you will conceive in your womb, and bear a son, and you shall name Him Jesus. He will be great, and will be called the Son of the Most High;

---

⁶⁴ Ps. 89:34-36 (35-37).

and the L-rd G-d will give Him the throne of His father David; and He will reign over the house of Jacob forever; and His kingdom will have no end." And Mary said to the angel, "How can this be, since I am a virgin?" And the angel answered and said to her, "The Holy Spirit will come upon you, and the power of the Most High will overshadow you; and for that reason the holy offspring shall be called the Son of G-d. And behold, even your relative Elizabeth has also conceived a son in her old age; and she who was called barren is now in her sixth month. For nothing will be impossible with G-d." And Mary said, "Behold, the bondslave of the L-rd; be it done to me according to your word." And the angel departed from her.[65]

Thus, G-d's Spirit touched Mary's body such that an embryo formed in her womb while she was still a virgin. Furthermore, not long before Mary's miracle, G-d gave a signal that He was returning to His pattern of miraculous births when He enabled Elizabeth to get pregnant. She was Mary's much older cousin, and she had been barren all her life. Like Sarah a couple of millennia earlier, G-d healed her body so that Elizabeth was able to conceive.[66] Then she and her husband had a baby. They named him John, and he would be Jesus' cousin. He would go on to devote his life to the will of G-d and he would die as a martyr. He came to be known as John the Baptist as he drew the attention of the nation by baptizing people in the Jordan River.

---

[65] Lk. 1:26-38.
[66] Lk. 1:5-25.

In conclusion, the pattern of miraculous conceptions in the Hebrew Bible that started with Sarah pointed to the conception of a special individual. He would have a unique lineage, and He would be righteous. It is Jesus.

* * * * *

Jesus' biggest detractors were the religious leaders of His day. On one occasion, following Jesus casting out a demon from a man and healing his blindness, the religious leaders questioned what Jesus did in a very insulting manner. They said He performed the exorcism by the power of the devil. Jesus responded very strongly and warned them that their eternal souls were in jeopardy. Then they said, "Teacher, we want to see a sign from You."[67] But Jesus had just performed a miracle when He healed the blind man who was demon-possessed. Therefore, He said,

> "An evil and adulterous generation craves for a sign; and yet no sign shall be given to it but the sign of Jonah the prophet; for just as JONAH WAS THREE DAYS AND THREE NIGHTS IN THE BELLY OF THE SEA MONSTER, so shall the Son of Man be three days and three nights in the heart of the earth. . . ."[68]

So Jesus said no to their insincere request for a second miracle. Nonetheless, He prophesied that He would be the object of an extremely rare miracle. Namely, He would rise from the dead after being in the grave for three days. That's a pretty miraculous sign. In fact, once He perished after

---

[67] Mt. 12:38.
[68] Mt. 12:39-40.

laboring for several hours on the cross, the Romans verified that He was dead by thrusting a spear in His side.[69] Next He was entombed for three days. Then He rose from the dead, and He appeared to His disciples and many others over a period of forty days.[70] No doubt, had one of the religious leaders really wanted to know the truth about Jesus, Jesus would have appeared to him too. But alas, perhaps not all, but certainly most of the religious leaders were not interested, and Jesus let them go their way.

Jesus' resurrection was an undeniable miracle to all who saw Him in that state. But His miraculous conception was seen by no one. Only Mary knows for sure what happened.[71] So, both events are miraculous, but only one of them is verifiable. Yet both events are interrelated and essential, for Jesus was born to die. More specifically, He came to die for the sins of the world. Christian theologians tell us that only G-d could accomplish this goal.[72] Of course, only G-d is righteous and qualified to pay the price for the sins of another, but also, only G-d has the infinite capacity needed to die for the vast sea of sins committed by human beings throughout history. Yet, He also had to become a human to be able to pay the price for the sins of humans. Hence, G-d devised this plan to provide for the salvation of mankind. Furthermore, He

---

[69] Jn. 19:34.

[70] Acts 1:3.

[71] Actually, Joseph also knew of Jesus miraculous conception as an angel appeared to him in a dream to reassure him in Mt. 1:18-25.

[72] e.g. C. Donald Cole, *Basic Christian Faith* (Westchester, Il.: Crossway books, 1985) chapters 18, 20, and 22; Jerry Bridges and Bob Bevington, *The Bookends of the Christian Life* (Wheaton Il.: Crossway Books, 2009) ch. 1; A. W. Tozer, *The Attributes of God* (Camp Hill, Pa: Christian Publications, 1997) ch. 4; L. S. Chafer, revised by John F. Walvoord, *Major Bible Themes* (Grand Rapids: Zondervan Publishing House, 1974) chapters 8, 9, and 28; et.al.

predicted both the birth and death of Jesus through His prophets. Then Jesus came down to earth and accomplished G-d's plan. In order for Him to take the form of a man, His birth had to be miraculous. Simply put, G-d could not be born through the union of a man and a woman. For He already existed. Therefore, there had to be a miracle. Hence, G-d selected Mary, who was chaste, to be the mother.

18

THE MINISTRY OF THE MESSIAH

There are two main subjects in the prophecy of the Hebrew Bible. One has to do with G-d's judgement upon the sinful Jewish people. This judgement would take the form of being sent into exile. Furthermore, the Bible foretold that the Jews would face this judgment two times. The second major subject of prophecy has to do with a very special person who would be born to the Jews and yet who would also somehow be G-d! He would be the savior of the Jewish people, and indeed, of all people. The prophecies of this special person were somewhat unclear in regards to the timing of His accomplishment of all of the different works that would be set before Him. In hindsight, it is clear to those who believe in Jesus that G-d's plan all along was for there to be two comings of the Messiah.

The prophecies of the first coming of the Messiah deal with His birth, ministry period, and sacrificial death. The subject of His birth was covered in the last chapter, and the subject of his death will be covered in the next chapter. In this chapter, we will take a look at prophecies from the Hebrew Bible dealing with the ministry He was to perform during His first coming.

In terms of the prophecies about the ministry of the savior, many of them have to do with His character. Such prophecies may seem subtle, but G-d knew what He was doing in giving us these prophecies. For, people can be identified by their behavior and their character. Certainly, everyone has a facade to one degree or another. But over time, people know who we really are. So too with historical figures, the truth about what they are really like always comes out in the end. For example, not only do we know that Julius Caesar was a great general, but we also know that his arrogance was enormous. We know that Ghandi was brave, principled, and humble as he proved it 365 days a year over the course of his whole adult life. Albeit, Ghandi was human and he did have some flaws. In the case of King David, we know that he was a great military leader and king, but we also know of his sins. In addition, we know what was inside of David. For not only does the Bible tell us,[73] but we know from his words and deeds that he loved G-d and he trusted G-d.

So too, the character of the Messiah would be distinct. Here are some prophecies of how He would treat people:

> "Behold, My Servant, whom I uphold; My chosen one *in whom* My soul delights. I have put My Spirit upon Him; He will bring forth justice to the nations. He will not cry out or raise *His voice*, nor make His voice heard in the street. A bruised reed He will not break, and a dimly burning wick He will not

---

[73] 1 Sam. 13:14; 16:7.

extinguish; He will faithfully bring forth justice. He will not be disheartened or crushed, until He has established justice in the earth; and the coastlands will wait expectantly for His law."[74]

Once again, Isaiah uses poetic phrasing to make the point more powerfully. He could have just said that this person would be gentle with those who are broken in spirit, but instead he phrased it in such a way to catch our attention. Notice also that G-d's Spirit would be upon this person, and that this person would not raise His voice to draw attention to Himself.

Here is a passage from the Christian New Testament about Jesus' public ministry:

> And as Jesus returned, the multitude welcomed him, for they had all been waiting for Him. And behold, there came a man named Jairus, and he was an official of the synagogue; and he fell at Jesus' feet, and *began* to entreat Him to come to his house; for he had an only daughter, about twelve years old, and she was dying. But as He went, the multitudes were pressing against Him.
>
> And a woman who had a hemorrhage for twelve years, and could not be healed by anyone, came up behind Him, and touched the fringe of His cloak; and immediately her hemorrhage stopped. And Jesus said, "Who is the one who touched Me?" And while they were all denying it, Peter said, "Master, the multitudes are crowding and pressing upon

---

[74] Isa. 42:1-4.

You." But Jesus said, "Someone did touch Me, for I was aware that power had gone out of Me." And when the woman saw that she had not escaped notice, she came trembling and fell down before Him, and declared in the presence of all the people the reason why she had touched Him, and how she had been immediately healed. And He said to her, "Daughter, your faith has made you well; go in peace."[75]

Have you ever seen footage of the Beatles early in their career when a throng of young women were pressing in to try to touch them as they were rushing to get into a car? Early in Jesus' ministry, He was getting a similar reaction from the Jewish people. Of course, the difference was that Jesus was not being chased by starstruck, screaming young women, but rather by people who were dying of diseases or suffering from physical conditions for which there was no cure in the ancient world. These poor people were desperate; Jesus was full of G-d's Spirit and He was healing them. Hence, enormous crowds were pursuing Him. However, getting attention was not Jesus' goal. It was just a consequence of His ministry. In fact, Jesus tried to tamp down the clamor, but that was hard to do. For the people He healed could not contain their exuberance and it attracted other people to Him.[76] Nonetheless, it is not the case that He was a self-promoter. He did not come in order to be loved by the masses. He came to help people find G-d.

In this event, He was on His way to help the synagogue official's daughter when this poor woman touched His robe.

---

[75] Lk. 8:40-48.
[76] Mk.1:40-45; 7:31-37.

Coincidentally, she had been suffering for as long as the man's daughter had been alive. Commentators tell us that she would have been ceremonially unclean, and therefore she would have been a social outcast.[77] So not only was she suffering physically, but also socially and emotionally. Ancient Israel was not like modern America where we have warm, cozy houses with electronics in which to retreat from the world. In ancient Israel, your position in society was everything, and this poor, suffering woman had lost that along with her health. She would have been broken. Somehow, she heard about Jesus. Perhaps she knew someone who had a family member who was healed by Jesus. Maybe she saw Him healing people, or maybe she just heard about Him. Now she was in a crowd and He was walking towards her. So she took a chance, reached out, and touched His robe.

She was healed instantly. Jesus stopped and said, "Who is the one who touched Me?" He was not going to move on, and she could see that. So she stepped forward and admitted it. Of course, Jesus knew all along who touched His robe. But He wanted to give her dignity by letting her come forward and admit it on her own. Then He acknowledged that it was because of her faith in G-d that He healed her. Did she approach G-d perfectly? Probably not. But she reached out to G-d for help, and that is all He is looking for from us. Jesus wanted her to know that G-d healed her because that is who G-d is. She did not take anything, but rather she was healed knowingly by G-d who cared for her. Jesus wanted to restore not only her health, but also her broken spirit.

In this story, we see the person Isaiah so eloquently described as one who would not break a reed that is bruised.

---

[77] John F. Walvoord and Roy B. Zuck, eds., *The Bible Knowledge Commentary*, New Testament Edition (Wheaton Il.: Victor Books, 1983) 227.

Jesus was gentle and caring. He did not put people down; He lifted them up. In Jesus, we see G-d's heart of compassion for those who are suffering. Jesus' heart was moved as He gazed upon people in pain, and He acted to help them.[78] In the case of this woman, Jesus was on His way to help a young girl who was near death when a large crowd of people began pressing in on Him. Despite the lack of personal space, Jesus paused to help this woman.

Incidentally, Jesus went on to raise the official's daughter from the dead as she passed away before He could get to her.[79]

Here is another interesting passage from the book of Isaiah about this special servant:

> "Who has believed our message? And to whom has the arm of the L-rd been revealed? For He grew up before Him like a tender shoot, and like a root out of parched ground: He has no *stately* form or majesty that we should look upon Him, nor appearance that we should be attracted to Him. He was despised and forsaken of men, a man of sorrows, and acquainted with grief; and like one from whom men hide their face, He was despised, and we did not esteem Him."[80]

Here we have a paradox. The arm of G-d is an idiom that means G-d's might. Yet, this one's life would not be a display of G-d's power. This person would not look like someone society would normally select to be their leader. On the contrary, He would grow up like "a root out of parched ground," perhaps meaning that He would grow up poor. Sure

---

[78] Mk. 1:40-42.

[79] Lk. 8:49-56.

[80] Isa. 53:1-4.

enough, Jesus did not grow up in a palace. Furthermore, the nation's final verdict on Jesus was exactly as predicted here: they did not esteem Him. Again, in the first line of this prophecy, and in other prophecies, it is foretold that G-d's chosen one will exercise G-d's might and judge the nations. But that is not what Jesus did, and nor is that what most of this prophecy is predicting. Simply put, there are two distinct parts of the special one's mission, and He has to come twice in order to complete them both.

Just before Jesus took His last breath on the cross, He said: "It is finished."[81] For He had completed the first half of His mission. So too, He will return and fulfill the prophecy pertaining to His victory over the forces of evil at the end of time.

It should also be noted that not only did Jesus grow up poor, but He remained that way for the rest of His life. In fact, Jesus did not pursue any of the rewards of this world that those at the top seek. He did not pursue or gain wealth, sex, rich food and wine, or control over others. Indeed, He had fame and power offered to Him on a silver platter, but He cast it aside. For at the height of His popularity, the masses sought to make Him king, but His response was to withdraw from the crowds.[82]

In terms of Jesus' ministry of healing people's diseases and physical conditions, that was predicted in Isaiah chapter 35:

> "Say to those with anxious heart, "Take courage, fear not. Behold, your G-d will come with vengeance; the recompense of G-d will come, but He will save you." Then the eyes of

---

[81] Jn. 19:30.
[82] Jn. 6:15.

> the blind will be opened, and the ears of the
> deaf will be unstopped. Then the lame will
> leap like a deer, and the tongue will shout for
> joy. For waters will break forth in the
> wilderness and streams in the Arabah."[83]

The context of this prophecy is the coming of the Messiah at the end of time. Yet, this detail of the Messiah healing people's disabilities is one that applies to both comings of the Messiah. Jesus healed countless people who came to Him with their infirmities. So too, when He comes back to retrieve the nation from all over the world and restore them to their land, He will do this same marvelous work again.

During Jesus' ministry period, John the Baptist was thrown in jail for speaking out against Herod Antipas, the tetrarch or ruler over a quarter of Judea. Herod was a son of Herod the Great, and John criticized him because he was having an illicit relationship with his sister-in-law, Herodias.[84] Once John was thrown in jail and potentially facing death, his spirit was down, and he started to question his ministry. So he sent his disciples to Jesus to verify that He was the Messiah. Jesus told them to tell John that He was fulfilling what was written in Isaiah 35:5-6. Namely, He was healing the blind, deaf, lame, and those with leprosy. He was also raising the dead and preaching good news to the poor.[85] Jesus knew this would satisfy John that He was indeed the promised one. For He was doing the works of G-d in the power of G-d's Spirit. Evidently, John had become confused by the ambiguity in the prophecies regarding how the two contrasting parts of the Messiah's mission fit together. After

---

[83] Isa. 35:4-6.
[84] Mt. 14:1-12.
[85] Mt. 11:2-6.

all, if Jesus was G-d's chosen one, why wasn't He establishing His rule over the entire world, and why would any of Jesus' supporters be fearing for their lives in jail as he was? Jesus did not send John understanding as to the mystery of the two comings of the Messiah, but He did send him a message that reassured him that He was the Messiah. John needed to have faith that G-d was in control and there was a reason why Jesus' ministry was unfolding the way it was. And John did. Jesus' message also gave John peace that his ministry was not in vain and that G-d would use it to advance His will.

There is another John in the Christian New Testament, Jesus' disciple John. He was very close to Jesus, and he wrote The Gospel According to John. In chapter 1, he wrote poetically about Jesus' divinity, and he called Jesus the "Word." Then in verse 14 he wrote:

> And the Word became flesh, and dwelt among us, and we beheld His glory, glory as of the only begotten from the Father, full of grace and truth.

In this verse, John is making the case that Jesus was G-d who came to earth and lived as a human. Jesus did not just give us a message; He was the message. He was a revelation of G-d. Albeit, in Jesus we did not see G-d in His glory, but in the form of a man. And yet, His glory was on display, and those who were open to G-d saw it. For they saw His character and it was beautiful. Jesus disciples spent seven days a week with Him for over three years. They wrote about His character in the four gospels that appear in the Christian New Testament. In the gospels, we learn that Jesus was accepting of all. He was patient, kind, caring, selfless, gentle, and forgiving. He had wisdom, He was honest, and He was without sin. He was also strong, and He exhibited righteous anger against profiteers on the Temple grounds who were misrepresenting G-d.[86] Finally, He was exceedingly brave. In Isaiah, we are told that G-d possesses this unusual combination of character qualities that people saw in Jesus:

> Behold, the L-rd G-d will come with might, with His arm ruling for Him. Behold, His reward is with Him, and His recompense before Him. Like a shepherd He will tend His flock, In his arm He will gather the lambs, and carry *them* in His bosom; He will gently lead the nursing *ewes*.[87]

In His conversations with individual people, and in His addresses to large crowds, Jesus taught spiritual truth. In His actions and in the way He treated people, He revealed to us what G-d is really like. Here is another example of the way Jesus interacted with people:

> And He entered and was passing through Jericho. And behold, there was a man called by the name of Zaccheus; and he was a chief tax-gatherer, and he was rich. And he was trying to see who Jesus was, and he was unable because of the crowd, for he was small in stature. And he ran on ahead and climbed up into a sycamore tree in order to see Him, for He was about to pass through that way. And when Jesus came to the place, He looked up and said to him, "Zaccheus, hurry and come down, for today I must stay at your house." And he hurried and came down, and

---

[86] Jn. 2:13-16.
[87] Isa. 40:10-11.

received Him gladly. And when they saw it, they all *began* to grumble, saying, "He has gone to be the guest of a man who is a sinner." And Zaccheus stopped and said to the L-rd, "Behold, L-rd, half of my possessions I will give to the poor, and if I have defrauded anyone of anything, I will give back four times as much." And Jesus said to him, "Today salvation has come to this house, because he, too, is a son of Abraham. For the Son of Man has come to seek and to save that which was lost."[88]

Here we have an encounter that was similar to Jesus' encounter with the woman with the hemorrhage, only Zaccheus had no physical infirmity. His desperate need was spiritual. He was a chief tax-gatherer. This meant that he was a traitor to his people. He was a Jew who collected taxes for the Romans and extorted additional money for his salary. The people who were under his jurisdiction could not refuse his demands because he had the power of Rome behind him. Thus, Zaccheus was a bad person, and he had no illusions about his standing before G-d. He knew that his immortal soul was in grave danger. The woman with the hemorrhage had heard of Jesus' ability to heal people. Evidently, Zaccheus heard about Jesus' message of G-d's forgiveness. So, like her, he showed up to see Jesus in person. There was a great crowd on hand that day as well. Unfortunately, Zaccheus was short and could not see over the people in front of him. So he climbed a tree in order to watch Jesus speak to the crowd. Of course, Jesus knew Zaccheus was in the tree. Therefore, when Jesus reached the point where He was beneath Zaccheus, He

---

[88] Lk. 19:1-10.

stopped and called out to him. Zaccheus had come to see if somehow G-d's grace could apply to him. Lo and behold, Jesus had come for him! This man joyously received Jesus' offer of salvation. For all it takes to be saved is to turn to G-d in humility and receive Jesus' offer of forgiveness. Hence, Zaccheus' eternal destiny was changed in the blink of an eye. He was so overjoyed that he gave away a great portion of his wealth in an attempt to right his wrongs and help the poor.

Jesus knows who you are too, and He is waiting for you to understand your need for forgiveness. Then He will come for you. I know because He came for me.

So Jesus came for outcasts, traitors, and even the hated Romans and Samaritans. But certainly, He also came for regular people, and Jewish religious leaders too. He came for all. Here is a passage where He interacts with a Pharisee:

> Now there was a man of the Pharisees, named Nicodemus, a ruler of the Jews; this man came to Him by night, and said to Him, "Rabbi, we know that You have come from G-d *as* a teacher; for no one can do these signs that You do unless G-d is with him." Jesus answered and said to him, "Truly, truly, I say to you, unless one is born again, he cannot see the kingdom of G-d." Nicodemus said to Him, "How can a man be born when he is old? He cannot enter a second time into his mother's womb and be born, can he?" Jesus answered, "Truly, truly, I say to you, unless one is born of water and the Spirit, he cannot enter into the kingdom of G-d. That which is born of the flesh is flesh, and that which is born of the Spirit is spirit. Do not marvel that I said to you, 'You must be born

again.' The wind blows where it wishes and you hear the sound of it, but do not know where it comes from and where it is going; so is everyone who is born of the Spirit." Nicodemus answered and said to Him, "How can these things be?"[89]

Nicodemus had high social standing. He had seen Jesus' miracles, and he knew in his heart that Jesus was from G-d. Evidently, he came to Jesus at night so that he would not be seen visiting with Him. Nicodemus wanted to understand Jesus' message of salvation. Jesus started explaining it by using a metaphor of being born again, but Nicodemus was still lost. Fortunately for Nicodemus, Jesus had the patience of G-d, and He would go on to explain G-d's grace and how it is that one can be saved. Included in Jesus' explanation are the famous verses John 3:16 and 17:

"For G-d so loved the world, that He gave His only begotten Son, that whoever believes in Him should not perish, but have eternal life. For G-d did not send the Son into the world to judge the world, but that the world should be saved through Him. . .."

Nicodemus appears two more times in the book of John, and it is clear that he became a follower of Jesus.[90] What about you? Have you read about Jesus in the Christian New Testament and somehow you know it is true, but you still have some questions? If so, you may want to follow Nicodemus' example and go to G-d in private and ask Him in prayer for understanding of His plan of salvation.

---

[89] Jn. 3:1-9.
[90] Jn. 7:50; 19:39.

* * * * *

The characters of the vast majority of rulers down through history contrasted greatly with Jesus' character. King Xerxes of Persia is a good example of the way most kings behaved. He is called King Ahasuerus in the book of Esther. In that story, he was in the midst of throwing a celebration second to none. He had invited virtually all of the princes, nobles, and army officers from throughout the Empire. During the celebration, he "displayed the riches of his royal glory and the splendor of his great majesty for many days, 180 days."[91] He really felt highly about himself, and he wanted everyone to see how great he was. The king threw a banquet during the final week of the celebration. Liquor was served, and at one point on the last day, he decided it would be a good idea to bring out his queen "in order to display her beauty to the people and the princes, for she was beautiful."[92] Not surprisingly, she declined.[93]

Here the king went to such great trouble and expense to celebrate himself, and when it was time for the grand finale, the queen embarrassed him in front of all the important guests. Immediately he summoned his team of legal experts to see what could be done. Needless to say, he punished her in order to regain a modicum of his dignity. But in hindsight, didn't punishing her just undermine his dignity even more? Wouldn't he have presented himself better by apologizing to her?

Her punishment was that she could never come into his presence again. Additionally, another woman would be chosen to take her place.[94] Therefore, a search was conducted

---

[91] Esther 1:4.
[92] Esther 1:11.
[93] Esther 1:12.
[94] Esther 1:19-21.

which ended in Esther being picked to be the new queen. Of course, the selection of Esther wound up having a great impact on the Jews living in the Persian Empire at that time.

The point is that King Xerxes was just another human king.[95] Seeking to have your greatness recognized does not make you resplendent. Jesus' glory was displayed when the Jewish religious leaders spit on Him,[96] the soldiers pounded nails through His hands and feet,[97] and the Jewish people made fun of Him as He experienced searing pain that lasted up until His final breath.[98] At no point on the cross did Jesus lash out against His adversaries. He underwent this injustice for our wellbeing. That is glory.

Indeed, G-d is not like us, and He does not think the way we do. His thoughts are higher than ours. It actually catches us off guard when He reveals His thinking and His plans to us. Here is a prophecy of the Messiah riding a donkey from the book of Zechariah:

> "Rejoice greatly, O daughter of Zion! Shout *in triumph*, O daughter of Jerusalem! Behold, your king is coming to you; He is just and endowed with salvation, humble and mounted on a donkey, even on a colt, the foal of a donkey. And I will cut off the chariot from Ephraim, and the horse from Jerusalem; and the bow of war will be cut off. And He will

---

[95] It should be noted that the kings of Israel and Judah were not much better than the Gentile kings. Certainly, there were some notable exceptions, but for the most part, the Jewish kings were petty and ungodly. For example, see Jer. 22:13-19 for an overview of the conduct of King Jehoiakim of Judah.

[96] Mt. 26:67.

[97] Lk. 23:34.

[98] Lk. 23:35.

speak peace to the nations; and His dominion
will be from sea to sea, and from the River to
the ends of the earth."[99]

Sure enough, Jesus rode a donkey down the Mount of
Olives to enter Jerusalem a few days before He would be
crucified.[100] Of course, the degree of difficulty in fulfilling this
prophecy was not very hard. Anyone could do it. Although, it
is doubtful whether throngs of people would bow down before
just anybody. Yet, in a deeper way, this prophecy does identify
Jesus as the Messiah. Similar to other prophecies dealing with
the character of the Messiah, in this prophecy we see that the
Messiah would have to be someone who held a very high
position and yet was humble. The truth is that people like this
are very rare in history, and this humility cannot be faked.

If you have seen the movie "Gladiator," or really any other
Hollywood movie about the Romans, there is invariably a
scene in which either a conquering general or the emperor
returns to Rome after having conducted an important battle
somewhere along the frontier. The welcome they receive is
magnificent. The emperor or general arrives on a beautiful
horse or a gleaming chariot followed by the army as well as the
conquered people in chains. There is a parade, crowds are
cheering, and there is much pageantry. A modern version of
this would be a ticker-tape parade in New York City held for a
group of astronauts, athletes, or war heroes. Even on film,
these ticker-tape parades are impressive. It must be very
memorable if you get to see one live.

But G-d's Messiah would enter the capital city in a very
different way. He would not be riding on the back of a
pedigreed thoroughbred. He would be seated on a humble

---

[99] Zech. 9:9-10.
[100] Mt. 21:1-11.

donkey. The day Jesus approached Jerusalem, there were no banners flying for Him. Furthermore, Jesus' means were humble, and he was not wearing any expensive jewelry or a gold crown. There was a crowd on hand as they were coming to Jerusalem to celebrate Passover, and they did recognize Jesus and cheer for Him. But it was for different reasons than are typically the case. He did not have a high position in the government, and nor did He lead the army in any battles. His fame came from performing miracles and teaching about the things of G-d. In addition, He was beloved because He exuded gentleness and kindness.

Thus, in the first verse of this prophecy, verse 9, we see a good description of Jesus' entry into Jerusalem. Verse 10 is a prophecy of Jesus' second coming when He will return at the end of history to put an end to war and establish peace on earth. This passage is another example of a double-reference prophecy. It combines elements of both Jesus' first and second comings in the same set of verses with no mention of the time gap that will take place between the two events. Understandably, prior to Jesus arriving on the scene, the Jews did not realize there would be two separate comings of the Messiah. But in the aftermath of the flurry of events consisting of Jesus' death, resurrection, and ascension, the time gap became visible.

It was a difficult time in Judea when Jesus arrived on the scene. The Jews were suffering under the Romans, who were brutal. In addition, there was much partisanship and conflict between the different Jewish political and religious factions. So, of course the Jewish people keyed in to the part of this prophecy pertaining to the Messiah coming as the arm of the L-rd to liberate them. But what did not catch their attention was verse 9, which really does not fit in with verse 10. In verse 9, it is a humble Messiah who makes His first appearance on the stage of history. In G-d's wisdom, it had to be this way.

Jesus will come back one day and put an end to the enemies of G-d and the Jews. But first, He had to come to deliver us from ourselves. Thus, two thousand years ago, Jesus came to pay the price of justice on our behalf.

19

PSALM 22

Psalm 22 was written by David. However, it does not resemble any event from his life, and nor was it prophetic of the way he would die. Rather, it is a prophecy about a crucifixion. David wrote this psalm around a thousand years before Jesus appeared on the stage of history. This prophecy would not have made any sense to David or the rest of the Jews at that time as crucifixion would not be known in Israel for another four hundred years.[101]

But once Jesus died on the cross, Psalm 22 became clear. Psalm 22 laid out in detail how Jesus' execution would take place, so that once it happened, people could read this passage

---

[101] Hal Lindsey, *The Promise* (New York, NY: Bantam Books, July 1984) 136.

and say, "Oh my gosh, this was predicted." Here are the first twenty-one (twenty-two) verses:

> My G-d, my G-d, why hast Thou forsaken me? Far from my deliverance are the words of my groaning. O my G-d, I cry by day, but Thou dost not answer; and by night, but I have not rest. Yet Thou art holy, O Thou who art enthroned upon the praises of Israel. In Thee our fathers trusted; they trusted, and Thou didst deliver them. To Thee they cried out, and were delivered; in Thee they trusted, and were not disappointed.
>
> But I am a worm, and not a man, a reproach of men, and despised by the people. All who see me sneer at me; they separate with the lip, they wag the head, *saying*, "Commit *yourself* to the L-rd; let Him deliver him; let Him rescue him, because He delights in him."
>
> Yet Thou art He who didst bring me forth from the womb; Thou didst make me trust *when* upon my mother's breasts. Upon Thee I was cast from birth; Thou hast been my G-d from my mother's womb.
>
> Be not far from me, for trouble is near; for there is none to help. Many bulls have surrounded me; strong *bulls* of Bashan have encircled me. They open wide their mouth at me, as a ravening and a roaring lion. I am poured out like water, and all my bones are out of joint; my heart is like wax; it is melted within me. My strength is dried up like a potsherd, and my tongue cleaves to my jaws;

and Thou dost lay me in the dust of death. For dogs have surrounded me; a band of evildoers has encompassed me; they pierced my hands and my feet. I can count all my bones. They look, they stare at me; they divide my garments among them, and for my clothing they cast lots.

But Thou, O L-rd, be not far off; O Thou my help, hasten to my assistance. Deliver my soul from the sword, my only *life* from the power of the dog. Save me from the lion's mouth; and from the horns of the wild oxen Thou dost answer me.

Displaying severed heads publicly to instill fear and coerce submission was a tool that empires used in the ancient world. But that was not good enough for the Romans. They preferred crucifixion. Although the Romans did not invent crucifixion, they took it to another level by using it rampantly. If a severed head could send a message, how much more so the sight of a victim writing in agony and screaming in pain for hours or perhaps even days.

With crucifixion, the victim was nailed to a cross. Sometimes, there would be a seat and a footrest. Needless to say, the seat and footrest were not for the victim's comfort as they increased the length of time it took to die. It could take up to three days.[102] Prior to their crucifixion, the victims would be scourged, or in other words brutally whipped until their backs were sliced open.[103] Then they would have to carry the cross-beam to the site of their execution. Thus, they would be paraded through the streets and subjected to public

---

[102] Merrill C. Tenney, Gen. Ed., *Pictorial Encyclopedia of the Bible*, Volume 1 (Grand Rapids: Zondervan, 1975, 1976) 1038, 1040-1041.

[103] *Pictorial Encyclopedia of the Bible*, Volume 1 1038.

humiliation.[104] Then they would be nailed to a cross. The victims did not die by bleeding out from the wounds to their hands and feet. Rather, their deaths came from being brought to a point of exhaustion while undergoing a prolonged state of physical pain. The victim would be affixed to the cross in a vertical position with their legs bent at an uncomfortable angle that led to cramping.[105] Cords were used to reinforce the connection between their hands and the cross-beam.[106] Their body would sag on the cross as their leg strength was compromised and their shoulder and arm muscles were not sufficient to support their body weight. The physiological effects caused by the sagging were a lack of oxygen and insufficient blood circulation.[107] So, they would labor to lift themselves in order to breathe. As they did, the tears in their flesh where the spikes entered their limbs would be stressed, causing ongoing intense pain. The end would finally come as either they would succumb to the prolonged state of physical trauma combined with blood loss and insufficient oxygen,[108] or they would undergo heart failure.[109]

It was awful. Can you imagine the anticipation of the crucifixion victim as they were carrying their cross-beam on the way to the place where they would get spikes pounded through their flesh? Cicero wrote, "Let the very name of the cross be far away not only from the body of a Roman citizen,

---

[104] *New Bible Dictionary*, Second Edition 253.

[105] *New Bible Dictionary, Second Edition* 254.

[106] *Pictorial Encyclopedia of the Bible*, Volume 1 1041.

[107] Frank E. Gaebelein, Gen. Ed., *The Expositor's Bible Commentary*, Volume 9 (Grand Rapids: Zondervan Publishing House, 1981) 184; and *Pictorial Encyclopedia of the Bible*, Volume 1 1041.

[108] C. K. Barrett, *The Gospel According to St. John*, Second Edition (Philadelphia: The Westminster Press, 1978) 555.

[109] *Pictorial Encyclopedia of the Bible*, Volume 1 1041; and Lindsey, *The Promise* 137.

but even from his thoughts, his eyes, his ears."[110] Yet, here we have it prophesied in the Hebrew Bible.

Up until verse 23 (24), David wrote these verses in the first person. But they were not about him. David never underwent any such grueling physical punishment.[111] In David's case, he died at a ripe old age. In fact, he had a strikingly beautiful young woman brought in to lie with him and keep him warm in his final days.[112] What can you say? It is good to be the king. On the other hand, David's selfish behavior towards this young woman has been recorded forever in the Hebrew Bible.

So even though Psalm 22 was written in the first person, it was not about David. But rather, a descendant of his would face this sentence one day. This poor soul would be poured out like water, and his strength would be dried up like a broken piece of pottery laying on the desert sand. In other words, he would be dehydrated and have cotton mouth. Furthermore, the experience would be so arduous that he would be disfigured by it and his bones would be dislocated from their sockets. David's descendant would have his hands and feet pierced by a group of evil men. In the end, he would perish from heart failure, or as David put it, his heart would become like wax and melt within him.

---

[110] Cicero, speech, "Pro Rabirio Perduellionis Reo," chapter 5, section 16, Henry E. Dosker, *International Standard Bible Encyclopedia,* ed. James Orr, Cross, 2022, https://www.internationalstandardbible.com/C/cross.html (accessed May 4, 2022).

[111] Ps. 22:15 (16).

[112] 1 Kings 1:1-4.

Surely, this prophecy describes Jesus' crucifixion as recorded in the Gospel of John:

> Then Pilate therefore took Jesus, and scourged Him. And the soldiers wove a crown of thorns and put it on His head, and arrayed Him in a purple robe; and they began to come up to Him, and say, "Hail, King of the Jews!" and to give Him blows *in the face*. And Pilate came out again, and said to them, "Behold, I am bringing Him out to you, that you may know that I find no guilt in Him." Jesus therefore came out, wearing the crown of thorns and the purple robe. And *Pilate* said to them, "Behold, the Man!" When therefore the chief priests and the officers saw Him, they cried out, saying, "Crucify, crucify!" Pilate said to them, "Take Him yourselves, and crucify Him, for I find no guilt in Him." The Jews answered him, "We have a law, and by that law He ought to die because He made Himself out *to be* the Son of G-d." When Pilate therefore heard this statement, he was the more afraid; and he entered into the Praetorium again, and said to Jesus, "Where are You from?" But Jesus gave him no answer. Pilate therefore said to Him, "You do not speak to me? Do You not know that I have authority to release You, and I have authority to crucify You?" . . . So he then delivered Him to them to be crucified.
>
> They took Jesus therefore, and He went out, bearing His own cross, to the place called the Place of a Skull, which is called in

Hebrew, Golgotha. There they crucified Him, and with Him two other men, one on either side, and Jesus in between. . ..

The soldiers therefore, when they had crucified Jesus, took His outer garments and made four parts, a part to every soldier and *also* the tunic; now the tunic was seamless, woven in one piece. They said therefore to one another, "Let us not tear it, but cast lots for it, *to decide* whose it shall be"; that the Scripture might be fulfilled, "THEY DIVIDED MY OUTER GARMENTS AMONG THEM, AND FOR MY CLOTHING they cast LOTS." . . .

After this, Jesus, knowing that all things had already been accomplished, in order that the Scripture might be fulfilled, said, "I am thirsty." A jar full of sour wine was standing there; so they put a sponge full of the sour wine upon *a branch of* hyssop, and brought it up to His mouth. When Jesus therefore had received the sour wine, He said, "It is finished!" And He bowed His head, and gave up His spirit.

The Jews therefore, because it was the day of preparation, so that the bodies should not remain on the cross on the Sabbath (for that Sabbath was a high *day*), asked Pilate that their legs might be broken, and *that* they might be taken away. The soldiers therefore came, and broke the legs of the first man, and of the other man who was crucified with Him; but coming to Jesus, when they saw that He was already dead, they did not break His legs;

but one of the soldiers pierced His side with a spear, and immediately there came out blood and water. And he who has seen has borne witness, and his witness is true; and he knows that he is telling the truth, so that you also may believe. . ..

And after these things Joseph of Arimathea, being a disciple of Jesus, but a secret one, for fear of the Jews, asked Pilate that he might take away the body of Jesus; and Pilate granted permission. He came therefore, and took away His body. And Nicodemus came also, who had first come to Him by night; bringing a mixture of myrrh and aloes, about a hundred pounds *weight*. And so they took the body of Jesus, and bound it in linen wrappings with spices, as is the burial custom of the Jews. Now in the place where He was crucified there was a garden; and in the garden a new tomb, in which no one had yet been laid. Therefore on account of the Jewish day of preparation, because the tomb was nearby, they laid Jesus there.[113]

It is noteworthy that Jesus had a very rough night before His crucifixion. Then the Roman soldiers scourged Him prior to heading out to Golgotha where He would be crucified. As He was carrying His cross-beam, He was in such bad shape that He broke down and could not carry it any further. A man from Cyrene named Simon was enlisted to carry it the rest of

---

[113] Jn. 19:1-10, 16-18, 23-24, 28-35, 38-42.

the way.[114] Hence, it is understandable why it only took Jesus six hours on the cross before he died.[115]

While on the cross, sure enough he became dehydrated. So they placed a sponge in a jar of sour wine and then lifted it up to him on a branch so that He could have a drink.

Also, it says that when Jesus died, a soldier stuck a spear in Jesus' side and both water and blood flowed out. In so doing, the soldier verified that Jesus was dead. In addition, the presence of both fluids appears to indicate that Jesus experienced a ruptured heart.[116]

The most explicit detail is prophesied in verse 16 (17), where it says: "They pierced my hands and my feet." Certainly, there is no historic practice other than crucifixion where one's feet and hands would be pierced. Again, the Jews would not know of crucifixion until four hundred years after David wrote these words.

It should be noted that there is a dispute over the word "pierced." In the Septuagint, or ancient Greek translation of the Hebrew Bible, "pierced" is a translation of the Hebrew word "kûr." Thus, Christian Bibles utilize the word "pierced" based on the Septuagint version of the Hebrew Bible.[117] In

---

[114] Mt. 27:32.

[115] Mk. 15:25-37.

[116] Leon Morris, "The Gospel According to John", Revised, *The New International Commentary on the New Testament*, Gen. Ed. Gordon D. Fee (Grand Rapids: William B. Eerdmans Publishing Company, 1995) 723-724; Lindsey, *The Promise* 137.

[117] The Pentateuch was translated into Greek in Alexandria, Egypt around 250 BCE. The rest of the books of the Hebrew Bible were translated into Greek to complete the Septuagint around 200 BCE; albeit, the historical information about their translation is scant. The earliest versions of the Septuagint that are available today date from the second century CE. (R. Laird Harris, *Inspiration and*

Hebrew Bibles today, which are based on the Masoretic Text, the Hebrew word is not "kûr," but rather it is the word "ka'ărî" which means "like a lion."[118] Also, it should be noted that the word "kûr" is actually better translated "dug, bored, or hewed" as opposed to "pierced."

Needless to say, Jewish theologians who are opposed to Jesus are threatened by the word "pierced" as it connects this verse to two sister verses, Isaiah 53:5 and Zechariah 12:10, in which other Hebrew words are used that are translated as "pierced." When fitted together, these three passages complete a puzzle of a crucified Messiah. Much is written by both Jewish and Christian theologians about the debate over this word. Please read their writings if you are interested in this debate. In my opinion, neither side has definitively proven which Hebrew word David used when he wrote this psalm. Nonetheless, it is the case that different versions based off of the two different Hebrew words developed over time. The reason for this bifurcation could be due to a scribal error (as there is some similarity in the Hebrew spelling of these two words); a well-intentioned but misguided error in interpretation/translation; or a nefarious alteration of the text in an attempt to deceive. We may never know how or why the two variants came to be. But hopefully, one day archaeologists will uncover evidence that reveals what the original Hebrew word in the text was.

One of the arguments against the Hebrew word "ka'ărî" is that it does not seem to make sense in the sentence. The

---

Canonicity of the Bible, (Grand Rapids: Zondervan, June 1, 1971) 68, 99-100, 145, 186.)

[118] Of course, the original autographs of the Hebrew Bible were written in antiquity. The earliest versions of the Masoretic Text that are available today date from the tenth century CE. (R. Laird Harris 96.)

sentence would then be: "For dogs have surrounded me; a band of evildoers has encompassed me; like a lion, my hands and my feet." That does not make any sense. Although, David does use predatory animals metaphorically in this psalm to represent his descendant's enemies. So it would be fitting for him to use the word "like a lion" in this sentence which is about these enemies. But if that was the case, wouldn't it have made more sense for David to write: "like a lion, they are attacking my chest and abdomen?" Certainly, in the ancient world, lions were not pets that curled up by your feet or nuzzled your hands to be petted. Therefore, even if the word "ka'ărî" is the correct Hebrew word, it may still mean the same thing. Namely, the violent act which the enemies of David's descendant were to perpetrate against him would be to somehow maul or mutilate his hands and feet. For, the words hands and feet are not in dispute.

It is from verse 11 (12) to verse 21 (22) where the execution is described. And it is also in these verses where the metaphorical references to predatory animals are made. Specifically, David mentions bulls, lions, dogs, and wild oxen. Seven such references are made in total, eight if you count the word "ka'ărî" in verse 16 (17). Predatory animals were widely utilized by Daniel in his prophecies to describe the Gentile empires because the metaphor was so apt. In addition, the term "dog" was a pejorative used by Jews in the ancient world to refer to Gentiles. Hence, David appears to be referring to Gentile enemies in this section of verses. Indeed, the crucifixion was carried out by Roman soldiers. Furthermore, this metaphor is fitting in that the soldiers did act like animals in their handling of Jesus.

Certainly, Jesus was mistreated by the Jews as well, even though they did not perform the crucifixion. Their mistreatment consisted of bringing false charges against Him and loathing Him.[119] Their part in this event is prophesied in Psalm 22 verses six (seven) through eight (nine) which come before David makes any references to predatory animals. Matthew records Jesus mistreatment by the Jews as follows:

> . . . And those passing by were hurling abuse at Him, wagging their heads, and saying, "You who *are going to* destroy the temple and rebuild it in three days, save Yourself! If You are the Son of G-d, come down from the cross." In the same way the chief priests also, along with the scribes and elders, were mocking *Him*, and saying, "He saved others; He cannot save Himself. He is the King of Israel; let Him now come down from the cross, and we shall believe in Him. He TRUSTS in G-D; LET HIM DELIVER *Him* now, IF HE TAKES PLEASURE IN HIM; for He said, 'I am the Son of G-d.'" And the robbers also who had been crucified with Him were casting the same insult at Him.
>
> Now from the sixth hour darkness fell upon all the land until the ninth hour. And about the ninth hour Jesus cried out with a loud voice, saying "ELI, ELI, LAMA SABACHTHANI?" that is, "MY G-D, MY G-D, WHY HAST THOU FORSAKEN ME?"[120]

Indeed, the Jews mocked Jesus precisely the way David predicted they would in the psalm. They made the physical gestures and spoke the words just as Psalm 22 predicted they would. In fact, so close were their jeering comments to the

---

[119] Mt. 26:57-68.
[120] Mt. 27:39-46.

wording in Psalm 22 that the translators understood the mockers to be quoting this psalm. But the Jews would have never done that because quoting this psalm would have authenticated who Jesus was. Rather, it is simply the case that the psalmist was given prophecy of their shameful words and behavior, and one day it all came to pass.

There is another detail in the passage from John on Jesus' crucifixion which is not of any intrinsic importance to this event, but it is unique. It was not a normal part of crucifixion for the soldiers to gamble for the victims' clothing. But in this case, they did. Either they sensed that He was a celebrity and that His tunic might be valuable, or they desired it because it was seamless. Rather than cut it up, they cast lots for it. Their actions were out of Jesus' control. But G-d foresaw that they would do this, and He included it in Psalm 22 so that we would know that this is a prophecy of Jesus' crucifixion.

In terms of breaking the legs of the two criminals, this was an option that was available to the executioners to expedite the death process. By breaking a crucifixion victim's legs, he would not be able to push up with them to alleviate the difficulty he was having breathing. In addition, the blows to his legs would contribute further shock to his body. Hence, the amount of time it would take for him to die would be decreased. In Judea, per the Mosaic Law (Deuteronomy 21:22-23), it was not permissible for a body to hang on a tree or a cross overnight. In addition, the Sabbath was approaching and the Jews needed to get the bodies down before it came.[121] Therefore, they broke the two criminals' legs. When they came to Jesus, He had already died, so the soldier did not break His legs.

---

[121] Walvoord and Zuck, eds., *The Bible Knowledge Commentary*, New Testament Edition 340.

Of course, it is no coincidence that Jesus was crucified at the time of Passover. Nor is it a coincidence that none of His bones were broken in the process. For as the instructions for the Passover lamb were given in the book of Exodus:

> ". . . It is to be eaten in a single house; you are not to bring forth any of the flesh outside of the house, nor are you to break any bone of it. . . ."[122]

The death of the promised one is very important, and therefore, there is much prophecy about this event. Among the corroborating prophecies to Psalm 22 is Isa. 52:14 which says:

> ". . . Just as many were astonished at you, *My people*, so His appearance was marred more than any man, and His form more than the sons of men."

This verse sounds eerily similar to Psalm 22:17 (18) where it says: "I can count all my bones. They look, they stare at me; . . ." Imagine what Jesus endured. It disfigured Him! Somehow, His ribs were protruding. Poor, wretched Jesus. It is my fault for I am a sinful man. He is so good; He went through this for me as well as for every other person who has ever sinned.

Surely Jesus paid a heavy price on the cross. Indeed, He bore G-d's judgement in our place. This is the point of the first (second) verse of Psalm 22. Jesus recited this verse and attributed it to Himself while He was on the cross: "My G-d, my G-d, why hast Thou forsaken me?"[123]

---

[122] Ex. 12:46.
[123] Ps.22:1 (2); Mt. 27:46.

Jesus had an unbroken relationship with G-d going back to eternity past. Jesus continued to be in a state of communion with G-d in His soul when He came to earth and lived as a man. But on the cross, that bond of love was broken. In verses 4 (5) and 5 (6), it brings up how G-d had delivered the Jews from their enemies over the centuries. However, G-d would not deliver Jesus from His enemies on that awful day, even though Jesus was innocent. Therefore, not only did Jesus undergo crucifixion, but while He hung on the cross, the constant state of unity and communion Jesus shared with G-d was severed. In that moment, G-d poured out His righteous anger, which is the response that our sins demand, onto Jesus. I do not understand how that worked, but that is what happened. The Jews plotted against Jesus, the Romans perpetrated the murder, and even G-d rejected Him!

But then it was over. After six hours on the cross, Jesus made His final statement: "It is finished!"[124] Then He bowed His head and gave up His spirit. These words are not a direct quote of the final verse in Psalm 22, but they go along with it. The final words of the psalm are: "He has performed *it*."[125] And indeed, He did; Jesus paid the price for the sins of the world.

There is a change in the second half of Psalm 22. There are no more mentions of anguish, mocking, or extreme physical suffering. In addition, the pronouns shift from first person to third person, and it is not always clear who the referents of the pronouns are. The subject of the second half of the psalm consists of people praising G-d. Interestingly, the group of people praising G-d is defined as all the people of the world. These people include Jews and Gentiles;[126] rich and

---

[124] Jn. 19:30.

[125] Ps. 22:31b.

[126] Ps. 22:23 (24), 27-28 (28-29).

poor;[127] and people from all generations as opposed to people from only one particular time or generation.[128] The reason they are praising G-d has to do with what happened in the first half of the psalm. Indeed, Jesus' death on the cross was for every person throughout all of history.

Of course, the Jews have not been praising G-d over the past two thousand years for Jesus' coming. They have suffered greatly over this period, and to a large degree, it has been at the hands of Catholics and protestants. In far too many instances, Gentiles have acted like animals and committed acts of horrific violence against the Jews. Therefore, it is a fair question to ask: how can this interpretation of Psalm 22 be correct?

In Volume 1, we considered Joseph's life and how it resembled Jesus' life. Here is one more similarity.[129] Joseph's brothers loathed him. He was the baby. He was their father's favorite, and he told on them and got them in trouble. Joseph also claimed to have a pair of spiritual dreams that portended that one day his brothers would bow down to him. They could not stand the sight of him. So they did the unthinkable: they sold him into slavery in a foreign land. But lo and behold, his dreams actually were from G-d. Sure enough, many years later, Joseph's brothers did bow down before him. But it was a good thing. For on that day, Joseph forgave them and received them with love. Furthermore, he had the means to preserve their lives from the famine, and so he did.

So too, the Jewish religious leaders loathed Jesus. Jesus challenged their message of approaching G-d through following the Mosaic Law legalistically. Jesus taught that the way to approach G-d is to confess your sins and ask Him for

---

[127] Ps. 22:26 (27), 29 (30).
[128] Ps. 22:30-31 (31).
[129] Eitan Bar 24.

forgiveness.[130] The people of the nation responded positively to Jesus. In fact, so much so, that the religious leaders were threatened by the response He was getting. Furthermore, Jesus made cryptic and yet bold claims about being the Messiah.[131] The religious leaders could not stomach Jesus, so they got rid of Him.

In the book of Zechariah, Zechariah predicts that when the Messiah comes at the end of time, it will be in a moment when the Jews are facing another existential threat. In addition, Zechariah predicts that the Jews will be shocked when they find out who the Messiah is, and they will bow down before Him, just like Joseph's brothers did all those years ago. Furthermore, just like the reunion between Joseph and his brothers worked out well for Joseph's brothers, so too, this reunion will work out well for the Jews. For when this moment comes, they will understand that G-d's plan called for the Messiah to come two times, and they will receive Jesus' forgiveness:

> ". . . And it will come about in that day that I will set about to destroy all the nations that come against Jerusalem.
>
> And I will pour out on the house of David and on the inhabitants of Jerusalem, the Spirit of grace and of supplication, so that they will look on Me whom they have pierced; and they will mourn for Him, as one mourns for an only son, and they will weep bitterly over Him, like the bitter weeping over a first born. . . .

---

[130] Lk. 15:11-32; 18:10-14.
[131] e.g. Jn. 8:31-59.

In that day a fountain will be opened for
the house of David and for the inhabitants of
Jerusalem, for sin and for impurity. . . ."[132]

So, it will be at this time that the Jews will receive Jesus
en masse. Then they will praise G-d, and then every aspect of
the prophecy in Psalm 22 will be fulfilled.

* * * * *

Have you ever viewed a great masterpiece in an art museum?
Depending how close you stand, the painting appears
differently. If you are close, you can see the texture of the
brushstrokes, but you may not be able to get a good sense of
the overall painting, and vice versa.

Up to this point, we have examined Psalm 22 in very fine
detail. We have stood so close to it that we could see each
brushstroke clearly. Now let's take a few steps back and
examine it in its totality. Here is what we see:

David identifies a group of enemies, and he repeatedly
depicts them as wild animals. This description paints a picture
of how they would act towards their victim. It also links them
to other passages in the Hebrew Bible in which predatory
animals are used to represent Gentile emperors and their
soldiers. The only direct act of violence attributed to this
group of enemies is the wounding of the victim's hands and
feet. Then they would surround him while he underwent this
event of overwhelming suffering. Further, the event would be
public, and there would be another group of people there who
would mock the victim as he suffered. Eventually, he would
become exhausted, his bones would become dislocated from

---

[132] Zech. 12:9-10; 13:1.

their sockets, and his life would drain out. Then he would be laid in the "dust of death."

This is a pretty good picture of crucifixion.

David identifies the victim as himself. However, this never happened to him. But it did happen to his descendant, Jesus. In addition, there are details in here that are not normal parts of the crucifixion process, but that took place during Jesus' crucifixion. For example, the soldiers did gamble for Jesus' robe. Furthermore, who else's crucifixion ever led to people all over the world turning to G-d and worshipping Him?

* * * * *

Needless to say, if Jesus was the actual Passover lamb who came to die for the sins of the world, then there would be much prophecy in the Hebrew Bible about His death, and so there is. For example, Isaiah 53 is another prophecy which lines up very well with a number of the details of Jesus' crucifixion. We will examine this prophecy in the next chapter.

20

ISAIAH

The book of Isaiah is very poetic, and it contains an important message. It reconciles the subjects of human sin, G-d's righteous judgement, His faithfulness to His promises, and His love and forgiveness. Isaiah is a prophetic book consisting of prophecies written to the Jews living in the southern kingdom of Judah. Some of Isaiah's prophecies are explicit,[133] and some of them are semi-ambiguous. All of them are purposeful. Here are the opening verses:

> The vision of Isaiah the son of Amoz, concerning Judah and Jerusalem which he saw during the reigns of Uzziah, Jotham, Ahaz, *and* Hezekiah, kings of Judah. Listen, O heavens, and hear, O earth; for the L-rd speaks, "Sons I have reared and brought up, but they have revolted against Me. An ox

---

[133] e.g. Isa. 44:28; 45:1.

knows its owner, and a donkey its master's manger, *but* Israel does not know, My people do not understand."

Alas, sinful nation, people weighed down with iniquity, offspring of evildoers, sons who act corruptly! They have abandoned the L-rd, they have despised the Holy One of Israel, they have turned away from Him.

Where will you be stricken again, as you continue in *your* rebellion? The whole head is sick, and the whole heart is faint. From the sole of the foot even to the head there is nothing sound in it, *only* bruises, welts, and raw wounds, not pressed out or bandaged, nor softened with oil.

Your land is desolate, your cities are burned with fire, your fields - strangers are devouring them in your presence; it is desolation, as overthrown by strangers. And the daughter of Zion is left like a shelter in a vineyard, like a watchman's hut in a cucumber field, like a besieged city. Unless the L-rd of hosts had left us a few survivors, we would be like Sodom, we would be like Gomorrah.[134]

Isaiah was G-d's prophet to the nation over a long period of time, and he wrote a long book. He was there through the reigns of four kings. The Jewish interest towards the things of G-d during Isaiah's time was essentially nonexistent. However, they did find room in their hearts for the deities of their pagan neighbors.[135] Not surprisingly, the end result of

---

[134] Isa. 1:1-9.
[135] Isa. 2:8.

casting G-d out of their society was a mountain of sin. Indeed, sin became socially acceptable, and their society went downhill. G-d sent Isaiah and other prophets to warn them about the disastrous consequences that would follow, but they did not care. They paid Him lip service and continued to offer sacrifices in the Temple. But their hearts were not in it.[136] That is a problem because G-d knows what is in our hearts.[137] One day, the Jews exceeded G-d's patience. They sinned so much that He had to disassociate Himself from their sin and judge them; and so He did.

In chapter 1, verse 18, Isaiah quotes a very interesting statement from G-d:

> "Come now, and let us reason together," says the L-rd, "Though your sins are as scarlet, they will be as white as snow; though they are red like crimson, they will be like wool."

This verse appears immediately after the first 17 verses in which G-d castigated the Jews for their sinfulness. For example, in verse 4 it says:

> Alas, sinful nation, people weighed down with iniquity, offspring of evildoers, sons who act corruptly! they have abandoned the L-rd, they have despised the Holy One of Israel, they have turned away from Him.

Thus, in verse 18, Isaiah is utilizing a paradox to catch our attention. On one hand, he depicts his society as one in which the people are living immorally. But on the other hand, he is describing a future state in which the Jews will be completely righteous. As with all paradoxes, the question raised is: how

---

[136] Isa. 1:10-15.

[137] Isa. 29:13-15; 66:18.

can this be? Surely, Isaiah wants us to ponder this paradox and pay close attention to find the answer as we read through the rest of his book.

It should be noted that there are two levels of righteousness. The first one could be called moral goodness or godly living. This level of righteousness would be characterized by trusting G-d and following the Mosaic Law. In the words of Isaiah, to live this way you need to:

> ". . . Cease to do evil, learn to do good; seek justice, reprove the ruthless; defend the orphan, plead for the widow."[138]

This is the level of righteousness G-d was looking for from the Jews in the covenant He made with them at the foot of Mt. Sinai.[139] Although no one is perfect, people are capable of giving honor to G-d, leading honest lives, and looking out for the needs of the lowly. But typically, only a remnant of the Jews lived this way during the 1,000-year period in which the Hebrew Bible was written. However, it should be recognized that strides have been made, and in modern Judaism, there is a beautiful philanthropic spirit and effort being made to help the needy.

The second level of righteousness is G-d's level, moral perfection. Isaiah discusses both levels of righteousness in chapter 1. G-d deals with nations based on the first level, and individuals based on the second level. It is the second level that is in view in verse 18. For in verse 18, Isaiah is introducing the idea that G-d would provide a solution to the problem of individual moral guilt.

Thus, the Jews faced existential threats as a nation from the Assyrians and the Babylonians due to their lack of fidelity

---

[138] Isa. 1:16b-17.
[139] Ex. 19, 24, and 34; Deut. 27 ff.

to the covenant they made with G-d. But so too, each Jewish person was accountable to G-d for their own individual wrongdoings. Both matters should have been weighing on the Jews' minds. Fortunately, G-d sent Isaiah, and he waded into all of these matters to provide them with answers.

It should be clear to each of us that we are not morally perfect. Isaiah dedicated his life to doing the will of G-d, and yet he was not righteous in the way that G-d is righteous. This became crystal clear to him when he entered the presence of G-d:

> "In the year of King Uzziah's death, I saw the L-rd sitting on a throne, lofty and exalted, with the train of His robe filling the temple. Seraphim stood above Him, each having six wings; with two he covered his face, and with two he covered his feet, and with two he flew. And one called to another and said, 'Holy, Holy, Holy, is the L-rd of hosts, the whole earth is full of His glory.' And the foundations of the thresholds trembled at the voice of him who called out, while the temple was filling with smoke. Then I said, 'Woe is me, for I am ruined! because I am a man of unclean lips, and I live among a people of unclean lips; for my eyes have seen the King, the L-rd of hosts.'"[140]

Immediately, this very godly man knew he deserved to be judged, for he was not like G-d. He had a heart for G-d, but nonetheless he was a sinner. Isaiah sinned with his words.

---

[140] Isa. 6:1-5.

How can our sins, that are scarlet, become as white as snow? Scarlet represents blood, and we are guilty of shedding it, if not literally then figuratively.[141] In the case of Cain, he murdered his brother, and G-d said to him, "What have you done? The voice of your brother's blood is crying to Me from the ground. . . ."[142] First, Cain improperly offered a sacrifice to G-d, then he became jealous of his brother, and then he became enraged and slew Abel. Finally, Cain attempted to lie about it. How could his grave sins ever be washed clean such that he would become righteous? Certainly, he could have repented of his sins and reformed his ways such that he never killed anyone again. But the stain of Abel's innocent blood would have still cried out from the ground for justice.

Herein lies our problem. We are not righteous and we are not fit to come into G-d's presence. We are likely somewhere between Cain and Isaiah on the sin severity scale, but wherever we are, it is not good enough. Much of the content of the Hebrew Bible touches on this dilemma, and Isaiah advances the discussion. In fact, Isaiah starts to address the issue of our sin in the very next verse following his epiphany that he was unrighteous:

> Then one of the seraphim flew to me, with a burning coal in his hand which he had taken from the altar with tongs. And he touched my mouth *with it* and said, "Behold this has touched your lips; and your iniquity is taken away, and your sin is forgiven."[143]

In this concisely recorded event, an angel touched the place where Isaiah sinned - his lips - with a coal. This coal may

---

[141] Isa. 1:15.
[142] Gen. 4:10.
[143] Isa. 6:6-7.

have come from the altar of burnt offering, where sacrifices are offered. Thus, it may be that Isaiah was forgiven for his sins thanks to another paying the price of justice in his place.

* * * * *

Most commentators break Isaiah down into two sections, chapters 1 through 39, and 40 through 66. The first thirty-nine chapters deal primarily with the subjects of the spiritual condition of Israel and Judah and the impending judgments they were both facing. In addition, there is much written in these chapters about the sins of the Gentile nations and the judgements that they would receive. The second section deals primarily with the subjects of salvation from individual sin and the regatherings of the Jews following the Babylonian exile and the Diaspora.

A good example of Gentile sin and judgement from the first thirty-nine chapters is the incident from chapters 36 and 37:

> Then Eliakim and Shebna and Joah said to Rabshakeh, "Speak now to your servants in Aramaic, for we understand *it*; and do not speak with us in Judean, in the hearing of the people who are on the wall." But Rabshakeh said, "Has my master sent me only to your master and to you to speak these words, and not to the men who sit on the wall, *doomed* to eat their own dung and drink their own urine with you?"
>
> Then Rabshakeh stood and cried with a loud voice in Judean, and said, "Hear the words of the great king, the king of Assyria. Thus says the king, 'Do not let Hezekiah deceive you, for he will not be able to deliver

you; nor let Hezekiah make you trust in the
L-rd, saying, "The L-rd will surely deliver us,
this city shall not be given into the hand of the
king of Assyria." 'Do not listen to Hezekiah,'
for thus says the king of Assyria, 'Make your
peace with me and come out to me, and eat
each of his vine and each of his fig tree and
drink each of the waters of his own cistern,
until I come and take you away to a land like
your own land, a land of grain and new wine,
a land of bread and vineyards. *Beware* lest
Hezekiah misleads you, saying, "The L-rd will
deliver us." Has any one of the gods of the
nations delivered his land from the hand of
the king of Assyria? . . .'[144]

As noted in chapter 16 of this book, Rabshakeh was a
spokesman for the Assyrians and perhaps a field commander
in the army as well. His role was to try to convince the Jews to
surrender and thereby save Assyria from having to conduct a
lengthy siege followed by a battle. Like the king he
represented, Rabshakeh was quite arrogant and disrespectful
to G-d. The Assyrians were known for their brutality. They had
been taking the cities of Judah, and now they were ready to
come against Jerusalem. So when the three Jewish
negotiators reported to King Hezekiah the menacing words of
the Assyrian spokesman, the king was dismayed. He tore his
clothes and covered himself with sackcloth. Then he sent
some leading men to the Temple to ask Isaiah to pray for the
Jews. Speaking on behalf of G-d, Isaiah sent word to the king
that this threat would pass.[145] Shortly thereafter, King
Sennacherib of Assyria became distracted by a disturbance,

---

[144] Isa. 36:11-18.
[145] Isa. 37:1-7.

and he moved his troops five miles to the north to Libnah. Nonetheless, Sennacherib sent a letter to Hezekiah arrogantly threatening the residents of Jerusalem. At this point, Hezekiah went to the Temple and prayed for G-d to save them from the Assyrians.[146] G-d answered the king through Isaiah. Here is the end of a fairly long statement by G-d followed by an account of G-d dealing directly with the Assyrian army:

> "For I will defend this city to save it for My own sake and for My servant David's sake."
> Then the angel of the L-rd went out, and struck 185,000 in the camp of the Assyrians; and when men arose early in the morning, behold, all of these were dead. So Sennacherib, king of Assyria, departed and returned *home*, and lived at Nineveh.[147]

Perhaps it is not such a good idea to blaspheme G-d. Needless to say, no more arrogant words were heard from Sennacherib as he dejectedly returned home. In fact, upon returning home, he was murdered by two of his sons and replaced by another one.

In this event, we see a miracle on the level of the parting of the Red Sea as again G-d singlehandedly took down a human army. In rare moments like these, G-d acts to accomplish His will in history and to reveal Himself to the world. However, we humans are so spiritually confused that we struggle to see Him, even in events such as these. Indeed, Sennacherib returned home and continued to worship pagan deities prior to his death.[148] But G-d's intention was for the Gentile nations to find Him for their sakes. As well, the Jews

---

[146] Isa. 37:8-20.
[147] Isa. 37:35-37.
[148] Isa. 37:38.

needed to wake up spiritually and begin to only worship G-d. G-d's statement is not very flattering. He was not delivering the city from the Assyrian army because the Jews had been faithfully following His ways. On the contrary, G-d was delivering them to display His power and advance His plan to rescue mankind. He was doing it despite their sinfulness. He was also doing it to fulfill the promises He made to David, for He is faithful.

The nation of Judah had an earlier wake-up call as well. A few short years before this event, the Assyrians conquered the northern kingdom of Israel. Prior to that taking place, Isaiah was given prophecy that Israel would fall to the Assyrians.[149] This should have been a warning to Judah that she was next; for although Israel was more sinful than Judah, Judah was bad too. For example, although Hezekiah was a godly king who tore down idols throughout the land,[150] other Judean kings, including his father, King Ahaz, worshipped them. Ahaz even went so far as to sacrifice one of his sons to a pagan deity![151]

Hence, G-d both sent this warning of Israel falling and performed the miracle of destroying the Assyrian army to wake Judah up spiritually. Despite many warnings from His spokesmen, the prophets, the call of sin proved too great for Judah and the nation simply would not follow G-d. Indeed, G-d pleaded with them to take note of the prophecy He was sending them. He called on them to use their minds to look and see that their idols were mere carved blocks of wood that were incapable of performing even natural functions, let alone supernatural ones like prophesying.[152] But the Jews did not

---

[149] Isa. 7:8; 8:1-8.
[150] 2 Kings 18:1-6.
[151] 2 Kings 16:1-4.
[152] Isa. 41:21-24; 44:6-20; 45:20 - 46:7; 48:1-8.

seriously consider His plea. Therefore, although they were able to last approximately 125 years longer than Israel, eventually they fell to the Babylonians, just as Isaiah predicted they would.[153]

However, not only did Isaiah predict the downfall of Judah to Babylonia, but he also predicted their restoration, for the Jews are G-d's people and G-d is faithful. G-d also predicted the downfall of a number of Gentile nations in the book of Isaiah. For example, in Isaiah 34, G-d predicted the defeat of Edom:

> For My sword is satiated in heaven, behold it shall descend for judgement upon Edom, and upon the people whom I have devoted to destruction. The sword of the L-rd is filled with blood, it is sated with fat, with the blood of lambs and goats, with the fat of the kidneys of rams. For the L-rd has a sacrifice in Bozrah, and a great slaughter in the land of Edom. Wild oxen shall also fall with them, and young bulls with strong ones; thus their land shall be soaked with blood, and their dust become greasy with fat. For the L-rd has a day of vengeance, a year of recompense for the cause of Zion. And its streams shall be turned into pitch, and its loose earth into brimstone, and its land shall become burning pitch. It shall not be quenched night or day; its smoke shall go up forever; from generation to generation it shall be desolate; none shall pass through it forever and ever.[154]

---

[153] Isa. 39:1-7.
[154] Isa. 34:5-10.

In the case of Edom, G-d's judgement would include massive human death as well as destruction of the environment. Further, the judgement was permanent. The Edomites would never be reconstituted as a nation. The reason for their judgement is given in verse 8. Namely, they were judged for their crimes against G-d's people. Of course, the Edomites were not only Judah's neighbors to the southeast, but they were also relatives. They were children of Abraham, too. They were the children of Isaac's oldest son, Esau. The Jews were the children of his younger son, Jacob. The Edomites' hostile actions against the Jews were not only crimes, but they were also a betrayal of their blood relatives and of G-d. For that, G-d judged them permanently.

On the other hand, the Jews were only judged temporarily, despite their sins being a betrayal of G-d as well. Assuredly, their judgement was very harsh, but it was not permanent. In the next chapter, chapter 35, Isaiah predicts the restoration of the Jews from their judgement:

> The wilderness and the desert will be glad, and the Arabah will rejoice and blossom; like the crocus it will blossom profusely and rejoice with rejoicing and shout of joy. The glory of Lebanon will be given to it, the majesty of Carmel and Sharon. They will see the glory of the L-rd, the majesty of our G-d. Encourage the exhausted, and strengthen the feeble. Say to those with anxious heart, "Take courage, fear not. Behold, your G-d will come with vengeance; the recompense of G-d will come, but He will save you." Then the eyes of the blind will be opened, and the ears of the deaf will be unstopped. Then the lame will leap like a deer, and the tongue of the dumb

will shout for joy. For waters will break forth in the wilderness and streams in the Arabah. And the scorched land will become a pool, and the thirsty ground springs of water; in the haunt of jackals, its resting place, grass *becomes* reeds and rushes. And a highway will be there, a roadway, and it will be called the Highway of Holiness. The unclean will not travel on it, but it *will* be for him who walks *that* way, and fools will not wander *on it*. No lion will be there, nor will any vicious beast go up on it; these will not be found there. But the redeemed will walk *there*, and the ransomed of the L-rd will return, and come with joyful shouting to Zion, with everlasting joy upon their heads. They will find gladness and joy, and sorrow and sighing will flee away.[155]

Here, we have a destiny that is everlasting like that of the Edomites, but it is of restoration as opposed to destruction. Thus, whereas Edom's land would be destroyed such that it would no longer be habitable, at least not to humans, the desert land of Israel will be transformed into a lush garden paradise with streams and pools. How can this be? G-d can do it. In this glorious restoration, human maladies like blindness, deafness, lameness, and mental disease will be eliminated! The frustrations of life will be gone, and people will experience lasting joy.

But there is also a warning in this passage. Namely, not everyone will make it there. It is not clearly spelled out how to get there in this passage, but some hints are given. The

---

[155] Isa. 35.

spiritually foolish and the unclean will not be permitted to go to the restored Zion. But the ransomed and the redeemed will.

Indeed, Isaiah chapters 34 and 35 are juxtaposed against one another as there are corresponding and yet opposing elements in these chapters. For example, in verses 8 of chapter 34 and 4 of chapter 35, it speaks of the L-rd's vengeance. But whereas in chapter 34 it will come upon Edom, in chapter 35, it will not come upon Israel. Another example can be seen in verses 13 of chapter 34 and 7 of chapter 35. In chapter 34, it says that Edom shall become "a haunt of jackals," permanently. But in chapter 35, it says that Israel, which would be judged and become a "haunt of jackals," would later be transformed into a lush garden.

This juxtaposition begs the question, why? Why do these two sinful nations receive such disparate treatment? The answer goes back to their two forefathers, who were twins. Esau was the older, and Jacob was the younger. They were the grandsons of Abraham through the child of promise, Isaac. Isaac was very special and so were they. Jacob understood that the one true G-d had picked their grandfather from all of mankind to use and bless in an amazing way, and Jacob valued that highly. He wanted to play a part in G-d's plan, and he wanted to receive those blessings. Esau did not care. Now that is not to say that Esau was not a nice guy, or that Jacob was an especially moral person. Actually, it was just the opposite in both cases. Esau was his father's favorite. He was masculine and he liked to hunt. After a long separation, he exhibited forgiveness towards his younger brother as he welcomed him back to their homeland, despite Jacob's treachery many years before. On the other hand, Jacob was a deceiver. He tricked his father into giving him the blessing that his father wanted to give to Esau. On another occasion, Jacob craftily seized on a moment when Esau was weak and hungry and served him a bowl of stew in exchange for his birthright. In fact, given the choice, I am not so sure that I would not prefer to live next door to Esau as opposed to Jacob. The moral flaw of Esau was that he did not care about the things of G-d.

G-d wants a relationship with people. But for there to be a relationship, it takes two. Esau was not interested but Jacob was. For this reason, the descendants of Jacob became the people of G-d.

Could it be that the Jews who will make it to Zion at the culmination of history will be the ones who, like Jacob, have a heart for G-d? Could it be that the "fools," who Isaiah tells us will not make it there, will be people like Esau who are enamored by the things of this world as opposed to the things of G-d? In addition, could it be that the way to enter G-d's presence is to be ransomed or redeemed by G-d? This appears to be the message of this couplet of contrasting chapters in Isaiah.

Throughout his book, Isaiah utilizes Jacob's name to refer to the Jewish people. Indeed, Isaiah uses Jacob's name forty-two times. It is interesting that the three other major prophets plus the twelve minor prophets use Jacob's name a combined total of fifty times. So the life of Jacob appears to be the lens which Isaiah was looking through as he contemplated the Jewish people and their destiny. In other words, the Jews will one day receive eternal blessing from G-d. Yet, it will not be because they are sinless, but rather because they seek His blessing and He gives it to them out of grace.

It should be noted that Isaiah predicted both the regathering of the Jews from their exile to Babylonia and from a much lengthier second exile in which the Jews would wind up being dispersed throughout the earth.[156] Isaiah toggles

---

[156] Isa. 11:11-13; 43:1-7.

back and forth between these two exiles. Theologians express that they are not certain which regathering he is depicting in every single passage. But we can be certain that he is prophesying about two regatherings as he states that explicitly:

> Then it will happen on that day that the L-rd will again recover the second time with His hand the remnant of His people, who will remain from Assyria, Egypt, Pathros, Cush, Elam, Shinar, Hamath, and from the islands of the sea. And He will lift up a standard for the nations, and will assemble the banished ones of Israel, and will gather the dispersed of Judah from the four corners of the earth.[157]

The passage presented earlier from chapter 35 is referring to the second regathering. The description in chapter 35 matches the restoration that will take place at the end of time and in no way resembles what it was like for the Jews returning from Babylonia.

As stated earlier, the second section of Isaiah addresses the subjects of individual salvation and the two regatherings of the Jews. In regard to both of these matters, there is a key individual who is discussed. He is called G-d's servant, and He would be responsible to accomplish key parts of the plan of G-d. Inexplicably, Isaiah introduces an element of ambiguity regarding this person. Sometimes Isaiah identifies G-d's servant as Israel, for indeed, G-d has a very important role for the Jews to play in His plan. But there are other times when Isaiah does not identify the servant, yet it is clear from the context that the servant is not the nation of Israel. But rather, Isaiah is speaking about a special individual. The passages

---

[157] Isa. 11:11-12.

about this person are called the servant songs. There are four of them including 42:1-9; 49:1-13; 50:4-11; and 52:13-53:12. The key way that we know this individual does not represent Israel at large is because this person is sinless. Therefore, this servant cannot be the Jewish people. For Isaiah continues to repeat his theme of the sinfulness of the Jewish people like a drumbeat throughout his book, including in the second section.[158] On the other hand, Isaiah writes of this individual:

> "The L-rd G-d has opened My ear; and I was not disobedient, nor did I turn back. I gave My back to those who strike *Me*, and My cheeks to those who pluck out the beard; I did not cover My face from humiliation and spitting."[159]

This person "was not disobedient." Not only that, but He obeyed even when G-d called on Him to do something that was extremely difficult and physically painful. G-d never instructed the Jewish people to perform a task like this. Furthermore, again, Isaiah's position towards the Jews of his day was that they were disobedient. For example, in chapter 30, it says:

> "Woe to the rebellious children," declares the L-rd, "Who execute a plan, but not Mine, and make an alliance, but not of My Spirit, in order to add sin to sin; who proceed down to Egypt, without consulting Me, to take refuge in the safety of Pharaoh, and to seek shelter in the shadow of Egypt! Therefore the safety of Pharaoh will be your shame, and the

---

[158] e.g. Isa. 59:1-8.
[159] Isa. 50:5-6.

shelter in the shadow of Egypt, your humiliation. . . ."[160]

Here is another passage from the servant songs about the special character of this servant:

"His grave was assigned with wicked men, yet He was with a rich man in His death, because He had done no violence, nor was there any deceit in His mouth."[161]

This person committed no violence nor told any lies. Isaiah never describes the Jewish people this way. In the verses leading up to this verse in chapter 53, Isaiah wrote:

"Surely our griefs He Himself bore, and our sorrows He carried; yet we ourselves esteemed Him stricken, smitten of G-d, and afflicted. But He was pierced through for our transgressions, he was crushed for our iniquities; the chastening for our well-being *fell* upon Him, and by His scourging we are healed. All of us like sheep have gone astray, each of us has turned to his own way; but the L-rd has caused the iniquity of us all to fall on Him. He was oppressed and he was afflicted, yet He did not open His mouth; like a lamb that is led to slaughter, and like a sheep that is silent before its shearers, so He did not open His mouth. By oppression and judgement He was taken away; and as for His generation, who considered that He was cut off out of the land of the living, for the

---

[160] Isa. 30:1-3.
[161] Isa. 53:9.

transgression of my people to whom the stroke *was due?*"[162]

Isaiah's use of pronouns is very deliberate in this passage. The pronouns include "He," "Him," "His," "us," "our," and "my." They are all either third person singular or first-person plural (plus one first-person, singular possessive). The first-person pronouns all apply to the writer, Isaiah, and his people, the Jews. Hence, Isaiah uses "us," "our," and "my people." This group is repeatedly portrayed as being unwilling to follow G-d's ways. Why does godly Isaiah include himself in the same group with the immoral Jewish people? He answered that in chapter 6 of his book. It is because he had sinned and was not perfect. The righteous individual Isaiah references in the third person is given the title of G-d's "Servant" in verse 11. In the above verses, He is repeatedly proclaimed to be the one who undergoes oppression, violence, and death in order to pay the price for the transgressions of Isaiah and his people. In fact, Isaiah calls the servant a lamb, harkening back to the innocent lambs that were sacrificed to spare the Jews from judgement on Passover.

In chapter 53, Isaiah uses the literary device of repetition. It is the blunt instrument of literary devices. Repetition is not elegant, but when something is of the utmost importance, it is employed to make sure there can be no mistake in what the author is saying. Not only is the message of sacrificial atonement repeated in these verses, but Isaiah goes on to repeat it a few more times in the following verses.

Although there are other places in Isaiah where the term "servant" applies to the Jewish people, it clearly does not here. Rather, it applies to a special, sinless person with a special mission to bear the sins of others. After all, one would have to

---

[162] Isa. 53:4-8.

be sinless in order to be able to pay the price for someone else's sins.

Obviously, this is Jesus. Jesus taught His disciples that His mission was exactly this-to die for the sins of the world.[163] Indeed, on the night of His arrest, Jesus quoted Isaiah 53 and applied it to Himself.[164] Then all hell broke loose. He said very little at His trials and He declined to defend Himself. He was scourged. He was struck in the face. He was spit on, and He was pierced. Then He died. Furthermore, once He died, He was buried in the tomb of a rich man.[165]

Returning to chapter 1, verse 18, how can we humans who have sinned and committed injustice be made as white as snow? There is only one way: Jesus had to come down from heaven, live a sinless life, and then give up His life to pay the price for our guilt. Once Cain struck Abel and took his life, he could not undo it. He could not make it right. But G-d could.

G-d's plan is wondrous. G-d is so good and so different from us that we do not understand Him. When Jesus came, He caught everyone off guard. Neither the Jewish religious leaders who had Him executed, nor His disciples who fled when He was arrested, saw this coming.[166] How absolutely preposterous Jesus' final act is to our natural way of thinking. Indeed, two chapters later in Isaiah, G-d acknowledges how vast the difference is between His way of thinking and ours:

> "For My thoughts are not your thoughts,
> neither are your ways My ways," declares the
> L-rd. "For *as* the heavens are higher than the

---

[163] e.g. Mk. 10:32-34, 45.

[164] Lk. 22:37.

[165] Mt. 26:57 - 27:60; Jn. 19:1-42.

[166] Mt. 26:55-68; 27:20; Lk. 24:20; Jn. 20:19-20.

earth, so are My ways higher than your ways,
and My thoughts than your thoughts."[167]

In order to understand G-d's plan, we have to keep in mind that our problems are beyond our ability to fix. Only G-d can fix them. Hence, the psalmist wrote:

> The L-rd is compassionate and gracious, slow to anger and abounding in lovingkindness. He will not always *strive with us*; nor will He keep His *anger* forever. He has not dealt with us according to our sins, nor rewarded us according to our iniquities. For as high as the heavens are above the earth, so great is His lovingkindness toward those who fear Him. As far as the east is from the west, so far has He removed our transgressions from us.[168]

In the last two verses of this beautiful passage, we see a confirmation of the message of the book of Isaiah. G-d's lovingkindness towards us is of heavenly proportions. He has separated our sins from us as far as the east is from the west. Recall that Adam and Eve were sent to the east away from G-d's presence once they sinned. But now G-d has provided a way for our sins to be removed from us so that we can come back into His presence free of them. Notice the common refrain between this psalm and the book of Isaiah that it is G-d who does the removing of our sins, not us.

In chapter 53, there is no mention of the Gentiles and their sins. However, praise G-d, there is at the end of chapter 52 as well as in the servant song in chapter 49:

---

[167] Isa. 55:8-9; c.f. 1 Cor. 1:18-25.
[168] Ps. 103:8-12.

> "Thus He will sprinkle many nations, kings will shut their mouths on account of Him; for what had not been told them they will see, and what they had not heard they will understand."[169]

and,

> "He says, 'It is too small a thing that You should be My Servant to raise up the tribes of Jacob, and to restore the preserved ones of Israel; I will also make You a light of the nations so that My salvation may reach to the end of the earth.'"[170]

The first passage is Isaiah 52:15. It is connected to chapter 53. The word "sprinkle" should sound familiar. Although it is only used twenty-three times in the Hebrew Bible, it is a very important word. It is the Hebrew word, "nāzâ." Nineteen of those times are in the books of Leviticus and Numbers. In these instances, "nāzâ" is used in regard to sprinkling sacrificial blood and/or anointing oil to either atone for sins or consecrate a person or an object. Thus, the word "nāzâ" fits in very well with the subject matter of chapter 53 in which the special servant of G-d sheds His blood as a sacrifice for the sins of mankind. But in Isaiah 52:15, it is saying that this sacrifice is for the sins of the Gentile nations as well!

Undoubtedly, chapter 53 is the theological crescendo of the book of Isaiah. The next two chapters deal with topics that reverberate outward from chapter 53. In chapter 54, G-d is dealing with the Jewish people as a nation and the subject is the final regathering of the Jews at the end of time. At that

---

[169] Isa. 52:15.
[170] Isa. 49:6.

time, G-d will restore the desert landscape of Israel. Furthermore, He will live there and have relationships with everyone there.[171] This can only happen if people are worthy to enter G-d's presence. Therefore, there has to be a special servant or savior who dies for their sins.

In Isaiah 54, G-d calls Jerusalem the "afflicted one" that has been "storm-tossed, and not comforted."[172] Indeed, this city and her people have been battered beyond recognition on more than one occasion. But once history runs its course, the Jews will be at peace with G-d and free from fear forevermore. Therefore, G-d also says in chapter 54:

> "For a brief moment I forsook you, but with great compassion I will gather you. In an outburst of anger I hid My face from you for a moment; but with everlasting loving-kindness I will have compassion on you," says the L-rd your Redeemer.[173]

It is beyond our ability to comprehend the concept of eternity. But one day, as eternity moves forward, the past four millennia of Jewish suffering will feel like it did not last very long, as awful as it was. Also, it is not possible for us to fully appreciate how good eternity will be. In eternity, G-d will extend "great compassion" and "everlasting lovingkindness" to the Jewish people. Throughout history, the Jews have been subjected to unspeakable violence and evil. It is hard to express or even comprehend the pain the Jews have undergone, and yet the Jews know it. What will it be like to receive love directly from G-d and to be granted the ability to give pure love? One day, the Jews will know that too.

---

[171] Isa. 33:17-24; Jer. 31:31-34.
[172] Isa. 54:11.
[173] Isa. 54:7-8; c.f. Isa. 51:17-22.

Isaiah chapter 55 is full of hope as well. In chapter 55, G-d reaches out to people as individuals. In chapter 55, the all-important information on how to receive the servant's sacrifice as a payment for your sins is revealed:

> "Ho! Every one who thirsts, come to the waters; and you who have no money come, buy and eat. Come, buy wine and milk without money and without cost. Why do you spend money for what is not bread, and your wages for what does not satisfy? Listen carefully to Me, and eat what is good, and delight yourself in abundance. Incline your ear and come to Me. Listen, that you may live; and I will make an everlasting covenant with you, *according to* the faithful mercies shown to David. . . ."[174]

What beautiful writing. What a beautiful message. How do you get G-d's provision for your soul? You cannot earn it, but rather, you buy it without money and without cost. In other words, it can only be received as a gift from G-d. There is a cost, but it was paid for by G-d's servant. How do you receive this gift? First, you have to come to G-d without any pretensions that you deserve His acceptance. For what you actually deserve is His judgment.[175] Then you simply ask Him for His grace. This is what Jacob did. Jacob wanted G-d's gifts and blessings. Like Jacob, you have to see the value in G-d's blessings and forgiveness. Thus, you have to loosen your grasp on the things of this world, and you have to forsake your sins and turn to G-d for salvation.[176] Isaiah also says you have to

---

[174] Isa. 55:1-3.
[175] Isa. 66:2; Ps. 103:11.
[176] Isa. 55:7.

listen. Listen to who? Daniel says you have to listen to the prophets, for G-d's message of forgiveness is there.[177] Another example of how to come to G-d is David. For David approached G-d in exactly this way. David's life was a paradox. On one hand, he was down with Cain near the bottom of the sin severity scale as he was an adulterer and a murderer. But on the other hand, he was high up on the godliness scale along with Isaiah as he truly loved G-d in his heart. So how did he approach G-d when he sinned? He asked for forgiveness based solely on the grace of G-d:

> "Be gracious to me, O G-d, according to Thy lovingkindness; according to the greatness of Thy compassion blot out my transgressions. Wash me thoroughly from my iniquity, and cleanse me from my sin. For I know my transgressions, and my sin is ever before me. Against Thee, Thee only, I have sinned, and done what is evil in Thy sight, so that Thou are justified when Thou dost speak, and blameless when Thou dost judge. Behold, I was brought forth in iniquity, and in sin my mother conceived me. Behold, thou dost desire truth in the innermost being, and in the hidden part Thou wilt make me know wisdom. Purify me with hyssop, and I shall be clean; wash me, and I shall be whiter than snow."[178]

G-d will not compromise justice. The price of justice must be paid for Abel's blood, Uriah's blood, and the blood that we

---

[177] Dan. 9:6.
[178] Ps. 51:1-7 (3-9).

have shed.[179] We can pay the price ourselves by going to a place where we will be eternally separated from G-d, or we can turn to G-d for His solution. David loved G-d and he wanted to be right with G-d.[180] Thus, he prayed for grace. In Isaiah chapter 55, G-d is warmly calling each of us to come and receive His gift of forgiveness. He mentions David and He is telling us that we should come to Him the way David did.

What do you say?

---

[179] Isa. 26:21.
[180] Ps. 51:11 (13).

21

JEREMIAH 31:31-34

The book of Jeremiah is similar to Isaiah. It is very long, and it covers similar material. Much of the book toggles back and forth between two contrasting topics. The two topics are: 1. the Jews' deep and prolonged failure as followers of G-d; and 2. G-d's faithfulness to the Jews. Jeremiah predicted that the Jews would finally fail so completely that they would bring judgement upon themselves. Surely, just as G-d waited four hundred years until the "iniquity of the Amorites" was complete before He passed judgement on them, so too G-d would wait hundreds of years until the Jews ignored so many moral stop signs that He had no choice but to bring judgement down on them.[181] For G-d to withhold His judgement any longer would have been for Him to compromise justice, and He will not do that. Hence, G-d removed His protection from the Jews, and they were defeated by the Babylonians and sent into exile. However, Jeremiah also predicted that G-d would

---

[181] Gen. 15:13, 16.

be faithful to His promises to the Jewish people and regather them. In fact, Jeremiah prophesied two regatherings, one from Babylonia after seventy years of captivity, and the other from across the globe at the end of time. The first regathering took place in 538 BCE for the Jews from the tribes of Judah and Benjamin. The final regathering will result in the Jews from all 12 tribes being restored to their land to live in a state of peace forevermore. Indeed, it appears as though this regathering has already begun!

Intertwined in this book is the personal story of Jeremiah. He not only lived during a difficult period for the Jews,[182] but on top of that, he was persecuted by his leaders and countrymen. In fact, he was loathed for speaking the words G-d gave him for the nation. In addition, another topic is brought up at the end of the book. Namely, the Gentiles also stand guilty before G-d for their bold rebellion against Him. Therefore, Jeremiah predicted G-d's judgement of a number of nations, some of which has already taken place in history, and some of which will take place at the end of time.

Thus, the book of Jeremiah paints a picture of the depravity of the Jews. Their inability to follow G-d's instruction to only worship Him was their primary problem. They were warned in the Law as well as by multiple prophets not to go anywhere near the false gods of their neighbors. But they would not listen. They gave up the honor of being G-d's people to be worshipers of the atrocious, imaginary gods of the ancient world. Indeed, the Jews even joined in with the Gentiles and engaged in the spectacular evil of murdering their children in sacrifice to the pagan deities. Furthermore, the Jews' involvement in worshipping pagan deities was not uncommon, but rather it was ongoing for centuries, albeit

---

[182] He lived both in the closing days of the Kingdom of Judah and in the beginning days of the exile period.

there were interruptions during the reigns of godly kings. In the words of G-d:

> ". . . For the sons of Judah have done that which is evil in My sight," declares the L-rd, "they have set their detestable things in the house which is called by My name, to defile it. And they have built the high places of Topheth, which is in the valley of the son of Hinnom, to burn their sons and their daughters in the fire, which I did not command, and it did not come into My mind."[183]

Although, there was always a remnant of the Jews who followed G-d. But by in large, from the poor all the way up to the governmental and religious leaders, the people rebelled:

> ". . . For from the least of them even to the greatest of them, everyone is greedy for gain, and from the prophet even to the priest everyone deals falsely. And they have healed the brokenness of My people superficially, saying, 'Peace, peace,' but there is no peace. Were they ashamed because of the abomination they have done? They were not even ashamed at all; they did not even know how to blush. Therefore they shall fall among those who fall; at the time that I punish them, they shall be cast down," says the L-rd.
>
> Thus says the L-rd, "Stand by the ways and see and ask for the ancient paths, where the good way is, and walk in it; and you shall find

---

[183] Jer. 7:30-31; c.f. Jer. 32:30-35.

rest for your souls. But they said, 'We will not walk *in it.'* . . ." [184]

It was an immoral era. The people were stubborn towards G-d, and they became treacherous:

". . . But this people has a stubborn and rebellious heart; . . ." [185]

and,

". . . For all of them are adulterers, an assembly of treacherous men. And they bend their tongue *like* the bow; lies and not truth prevail in the land; for they proceed from evil to evil, and they do not know Me," declares the L-rd. [186]

Here is a sampling of verses showing how the Jewish leaders treated Jeremiah on three different occasions. This is the reception they afforded G-d's spokesman whom He sent to lead them in the right way and keep them safe:

When Pashhur the priest, the son of Immer, who was the chief officer in the house of the L-rd, heard Jeremiah prophesying these things, Pashhur had Jeremiah the prophet beaten, and put him in the stocks that were at the upper Benjamin Gate, which was by the house of the L-rd. [187]

---

[184] Jer. 6:13-16.
[185] Jer. 5:23a.
[186] Jer. 9:2b-3 (1b-2).
[187] Jer. 20:1-2.

> So they went to the king in the court, but they had deposited the scroll in the chamber of Elishama the scribe, and they reported all the words to the king. Then the king sent Jehudi to get the scroll, and he took it out of the chamber of Elishama the scribe. And Jehudi read it to the king as well as to all the officials who stood beside the king. Now the king was sitting in the winter house in the ninth month, with a *fire* burning in the brazier before him. And it came about, when Jehudi had read three or four columns, *the king* cut it with a scribe's knife and threw *it* into the fire that was in the brazier, until all the scroll was consumed in the fire that was in the brazier.[188]

and,

> Then they took Jeremiah and cast him into the cistern *of* Malchijah the king's son, which was in the court of the guardhouse; and they let Jeremiah down with ropes. Now in the cistern there was no water but only mud, and Jeremiah sank into the mud.[189]

This is how much the Jewish religious and governmental leaders valued G-d's will and instruction. Tragically, all too often the people went along with them.

Jeremiah prophesied for a very long time. Eventually the Jews underwent judgement, and he was still around to see it. A small portion of the Jews were not taken into captivity in

---

[188] Jer. 36:20-23; The king was King Jehoiakim.
[189] Jer. 38:6.

Babylonia. Instead, they went to Egypt. Jeremiah was among them. Of all things, these Jewish foreigners in Egypt started worshipping pagan deities again! G-d sent them a dire warning through Jeremiah to finally learn their lesson and end their rebellion. Here is their response to Jeremiah:

> Then all the men who were aware that their wives were burning sacrifices to other gods, along with all the women who were standing by, *as* a large assembly, including all the people who were living in Pathros in the land of Egypt, responded to Jeremiah, saying, "As for the message that you have spoken to us in the name of the L-rd, we are not going to listen to you! But rather we will certainly carry out every word that has proceeded from our mouths, by burning sacrifices to the queen of heaven and pouring out libations to her, just as we ourselves, our forefathers, our kings and our princes did in the cities of Judah and in the streets of Jerusalem; for *then* we had plenty of food, and were well off, and saw no misfortune. . . ."[190]

G-d tried to warn them, but they were not interested in what He had to say. Indeed, it is hard to comprehend how great our capacity to rebel against G-d is.

Of course, the above passages are just some snippets of the moral and spiritual condition of the ancient Jewish people. It is advisable to read the entire book of Jeremiah to gain a deeper appreciation of their state of depravity. The two following verses are summary verses that illustrate how deep-seated our problem is:

---

[190] Jer. 44:15-17.

> "... Can the Ethiopian change his skin or the
> leopard his spots? *Then* you also can do good
> who are accustomed to doing evil. ..."[191]

and,

> "The heart is more deceitful than all else and
> is desperately sick; who can understand it?
> ..."[192]

We all know we are not perfect, but could it be that we are not fully attuned to how sinful we are? For example, how quick and how adept we are at defending ourselves whenever anyone is not pleased with us and gives us criticism. It is hard for us to see where we are wrong. But G-d, who is literally perfect, is capable of appraising our morality, and He says that our hearts are "desperately sick". The translation of the first verse above is a little bit confusing, but it means what you think it does. We can no more live righteously than we can change our skin color, or than a leopard can change its spots.

The truth is, the Jews' biggest problem was never the Babylonians, and nor was it the Philistines, Moabites, Assyrians, Persians, Greeks, or Romans. To be sure, all of those godless, ruthless Gentile invaders wreaked havoc on the Jews. But they still were not the biggest problem for the Jews. According to Jeremiah, the biggest problem for the Jews was always themselves.

However, there is more to the message G-d gave Jeremiah. Thankfully, the second major topic in Jeremiah is the antidote to the first one. G-d is faithful, and He will never fully reject His people. Hence, Jeremiah prophesied the Jews' downfall to the Babylonians, but he also prophesied that their

---

[191] Jer. 13:23.
[192] Jer. 17:9.

deliverance from the Babylonian exile would come seventy years later.[193] Of course, this deliverance was only for the Jews from the Southern Kingdom of Judah. But Jeremiah also prophesied another deliverance that will come at the end of time for the Jews from both the Southern Kingdom of Judah and the Northern Kingdom of Israel. This deliverance was predicted to be a regathering from multiple nations. However, Jeremiah did not prophesy the specific amount of time that the Jews would be exiled from their land prior to the final regathering. Of course, it is easy to trust that G-d will fully deliver the Jews at the end of time as we have seen Him do it before. G-d did this when the Jews were enslaved in Egypt. He did this seventy years after the Jews were hauled off to Babylonia, and He will do it again just as Jeremiah said He will.

But the Jews' biggest problem will still be there, namely themselves. Thus, one may ask why there will not be another exile after the next restoration. After all, if the Jewish people are like a leopard in that they cannot change their moral spots, then why will it work the third time? Fortunately, Jeremiah answers this question in chapter 31, verses 31 through 34:

> ". . . Behold, days are coming," declares the L-rd, "when I will make a new covenant with the house of Israel and with the house of Judah, not like the covenant which I made with their fathers in the day I took them by the hand to bring them out of the land of Egypt, My covenant which they broke, although I was a husband to them," declares the L-rd. "But this is the covenant which I will make with the house of Israel after those

---

[193] Jer. 25:11-12; 29:10.

days," declares the L-rd, "I will put My law within them, and on their heart I will write it; and I will be their G-d, and they shall be My people. And they shall not teach again, each man his neighbor and each man his brother, saying, 'Know the L-rd,' for they shall all know Me, from the least of them to the greatest of them," declares the L-rd, "for I will forgive their iniquity, and their sin I will remember no more."

A leopard cannot change its spots, but G-d can. Jeremiah makes a compelling, fifty-two-chapter argument that we are irredeemably morally broken. Oh sure, we can change some outward behaviors, and we should. However, we cannot change our souls. But G-d can. G-d can transform us so that our hearts are pure and we can love other people from deep within our souls.

Not only will G-d one day deliver the Jews from their human enemies, but He will also deliver them from themselves. Praise G-d.

* * * * *

One of the sub-themes in the book of Jeremiah is the godlessness of the Jewish religious leaders. For example, this theme comes up in chapters 14, 20, 23, and 50. G-d is strongly opposed to those who claim to represent Him, but who actually represent themselves. Lamentably, false prophets abounded in Jeremiah's day leading the people astray:

"... For both prophet and priest are polluted; even in My house I have found their wickedness," declares the L-rd. . . . "Also among the prophets of Jerusalem I have seen a horrible thing: the committing of adultery and walking in falsehood; and they strengthen the hands of evildoers, so that no one has turned back from his wickedness. All of them have become to Me like Sodom, and her inhabitants like Gomorrah. . .."

Thus says the L-rd of hosts, "Do not listen to the words of the prophets who are prophesying to you. They are leading you into futility; they speak a vision of their own imagination, not from the mouth of the L-rd. They keep saying to those who despise Me, 'The L-rd has said, "You will have peace" '; and as for everyone who walks in the stubbornness of his own heart, they say, 'Calamity will not come upon you.' But who has stood in the council of the L-rd, that he should see and hear His word? Who has given heed to His word and listened? Behold, the storm of the L-rd has gone forth in wrath, even a whirling tempest; it will swirl down on the head of the wicked. The anger of the L-rd will not turn back until He has performed and carried out the purposes of His heart; in the last days you will clearly understand it. I did not send *these* prophets, but they ran. I did not speak to them, but they prophesied. But if they had stood in My council, then they would have announced My words to My people, and would have turned them back from their evil way and from the evil of their deeds. . . ."[194]

This appears to be a double-reference prophecy in which Jeremiah is speaking to the Jewish people in his own day and at the end of time.[195] There were religious posers in Jeremiah's day claiming to speak for G-d. They found an all too willing audience in the Jewish people, and disaster ensued.

G-d did speak through Jeremiah, and others as well. But the people did not find their message appealing as it challenged the way they were living. Indeed, the Jews imprisoned Jeremiah.

What about today? Do the messages you are hearing from your leaders agree with the words of Jeremiah and the other prophets in the Hebrew Bible? The way to know is to read the Bible for yourself. Here is some wisdom on how to do that from Hillel Zeitlin:

> Let us again take the Bible and study it, as our forefathers told us to do: "With the understanding of the heart, with fear and awe, with humility, with joy, with purity," and try to forget the interpretations which estrange us from the plain meaning, rejecting all the distortions and falsifications of Biblical Criticism, . . .[196]

G-d's message in the Bible is understandable. He is speaking to everyone. Certainly, good religious leaders can help people spiritually. But in Jeremiah's day, the religious

---

[194] Jer. 23:11, 14, 16-22.

[195] Jer. 23:20.

[196] *Great Yiddish Writers of the Twentieth Century*, Translated by Joseph Leftwich, Written by Hillel Zeitlin, p. 64.

leaders were not good and they led the Jewish people over a cliff. Of course, there was always a remnant who knew when their religious leaders were misrepresenting G-d. These Jewish people put G-d's will first in their lives despite the errant spiritual direction promulgated by their leaders. Hopefully your leaders are godly. But it is possible they are not. After all, that has happened before in history. It is advisable to read the Bible, learn G-d's will, and put it first in your life. The question is not, Is the message in Jeremiah offensive? Surely the notion of a righteous G-d judging people for their sins offends people today. But rather, the question is, Is the message in Jeremiah true?

However, it is important to consider the message of Jeremiah in its totality. For it is not only a message of Jewish and Gentile sin and the necessity for G-d to judge our iniquities in order to uphold justice. But the message in Jeremiah also includes the notion of a loving G-d who offers us forgiveness and provides us with a solution. In the words of G-d:

> 'For I know the plans that I have for you,'
> declares the L-rd, 'plans for welfare and not
> for calamity to give you a future and a hope.
> Then you will call upon Me and come and
> pray to Me, and I will listen to you. And you
> will seek Me and find *Me*, when you search
> for Me with all your heart. And I will be found
> by you,' declares the L-rd, 'and I will restore
> your fortunes and will gather you from all the
> nations and from all the places where I have
> driven you,' declares the L-rd, 'and I will

> bring you back to the place from where I sent
> you into exile.'[197]

G-d is good. Perhaps it is time to "search for Him with all your heart." His plans for you are for your good. The regathering of the Jews has already begun, and surely, G-d is behind it. It may not be long until He completes it!

---

[197] Jer. 29:11-14.

22

DANIEL 9:24-27

It can be argued that chapter 9 in the book of Daniel is the lynchpin of Biblical prophecy. In verse 24, it says that G-d has decreed seventy heptads or sets of seven years to work through the Jewish people to execute His plan in human history. Six accomplishments that will be achieved through this union are mentioned including "to seal up vision and prophecy." Indeed, that is what Daniel chapter 9 is all about. It ties the entire Biblical prophetic program together.

In Daniel 9:26, a most amazing thing is prophesied. It says, "the Messiah will be cut off and have nothing." In the Hebrew Bible, to be "cut off" can mean to be killed. For example, the term is used in this way in Isaiah 53:8 where it speaks of G-d's servant being "cut off out of the land of the living." Why would G-d's plan include His Messiah being killed? How could that accomplish His will? For certainly, the accomplishment of G-d's will is the subject of Daniel chapter 9. Therefore, somehow the absurd proposition of

G-d's Messiah being killed must fit into G-d's overall rescue plan for humanity.

Daniel wrote his book after being taken hostage to the city of Babylon while he was still a youth.[198] There were three stages in which Babylonia conquered the Jews. The first two were relatively peaceful as the Jews capitulated. The third and final one was excruciating for the Jews as they resisted and the Babylonians unleashed hell upon them. Daniel was taken from Israel to Babylon during the first stage. He had a heart for G-d and he was even willing to die for his faith.[199] Daniel loved G-d, the nation of Israel, Jerusalem, and the Temple.[200]

Thus, Daniel wrote his book during a time of defeat and exile for the Jewish people. The root cause of these circumstances was the sin of the nation. White collar sin, petty sin, violent sin, heinous evil, disrespect for G-d - the Jews were guilty of it all. Furthermore, their guilt stretched back for centuries. They had been warned time and again. A large portion of the Hebrew Bible consists of prophetic warnings they received to stop before it was too late. But they could not help themselves. Finally, the day came, and they wound up enslaved in Babylonia while Jerusalem and the Temple lay in ruins.

Conjoined with the theme of Jewish sin in the book of Daniel is the theme of Gentile sin manifested by a string of ruthless empires. Daniel's prophecies of these empires highlighted the following features: power-lust, wanton violence, and blasphemous leaders.[201] Interwoven with

---

[198] Dan. 1:4-6.

[199] Dan. 1:8-13; 6:1 (2)-28 (29).

[200] Dan. 9:1-19.

[201] There are two graphic examples of arrogant kings recorded in the book of Daniel. The first one is the case of King Nebuchadnezzar erecting a 90-foot-high gold image in his own honor in chapter 3.

Daniel's account of human sin is a contrasting depiction of G-d's righteousness, humility, and graciousness. Furthermore, it is brought out in the book that although G-d has granted humanity free reign on the earth, there will come a day when He will put a stop to human sin. For, one day, His judgement will fall on the Gentiles and He will end their kingdoms forever.

All of these themes are easily identifiable in the book of Daniel. This book reveals the meaning of history from G-d's perspective. Yet, Daniel was a prophet, and although the content of his book is largely history to us today, he was writing about the future!

In fact, the book of Daniel consists of vivid prophecy covering the broad expanse of human history from Daniel's day forward to the end of history. It covers the four great empires that were to take place one after the other up to and including the Roman Empire. The first empire would conquer Israel and the final three would occupy it and oppress the Jewish people. Of course, the Jews were deported in 70 CE during the reign of the Roman Empire, and there they stayed for nearly two thousand years. Daniel's prophetic presentation of Gentile history fast forwards from the Roman Empire to the end of time when a reconstituted version of the Roman Empire will emerge. At that time, the Romans will again oppress the Jewish people who will have also rearisen as a nation and be living in their land.

After all these years, the Jews are back in their land again! Who would have ever thought that could happen in light of the

---

The other example takes place in chapter 5 where King Belshazzar throws a party just hours before his city would be invaded. At the party, he ordered that the gold and silver vessels that were seized from the Jewish Temple be brought out for the partygoers to use to toast their pagan deities.

unprecedented level of hatred and violence inflicted upon them over the past two thousand years? Daniel did, for G-d showed him. But today, we are still not at the very end of time, for Daniel tells us the Roman Empire will rearise, and that has not happened yet. Of course, the Temple has not been rebuilt yet either. It is hard to imagine how that will ever happen in light of the unrelenting conflict between the Jews and the Palestinians. For, the Palestinians currently have two mosques occupying the site of the Temple. But we know that time will tell and Daniel's final prophecies will come true just as his other ones concerning the Babylonians, Medes and Persians, Greeks, and Romans already have.

Except for chapter 9, Daniel's prophecies cover Gentile history. Specifically, they predict the Gentile empires that would impact the nation of Israel. But chapter 9 is about Jewish history, and it covers the time period following the Babylonian exile up to the end of human history.

In chapter 4 of Volume 1, the difference in the way G-d views human empires versus the way we do was discussed. We see them as great human achievements worthy of being memorialized. For example, we pay homage today to the achievements of the Roman Empire. G-d sees these empires as brutal beasts bent on world conquest and self-aggrandizement. Certainly, He is right. Each new attempt at world takeover bears the fingerprints of all the ones that came before. It does not matter whether it was the Germans in World War II, or the Greeks in the fourth century BCE. At the heart of it, the motivations and the will to use violence have always been the same. However, there is a difference today in that technology and the ability to inflict destruction have increased tremendously. Another common feature of world takeover attempts, and world history in general, is the singling out of the Jewish people for special hatred, violence, and oppression. On occasion, rulers would even go so far as to call out G-d Himself! In fact, this rare and brazen act comes up in the prophecy of Daniel 9.

Let us not glance too quickly at the "better" world conquerors, such as Julius Caesar, and miss what G-d sees. The root sin of would-be world rulers is arrogance. Why would anybody think that they have a right to build an army, launch a war against their neighbor, conquer them, and then subjugate them? It is immoral. But it is the way of the world, and it is the way nations have conducted themselves throughout history. Julius Caesar and the Romans won. Today, he is viewed as a great conqueror. Our month of July is named after him. But how would he be viewed if the Romans lost? It is likely he would be remembered for the atrocities he presided over, much like the other monsters of history. How breathtakingly arrogant and off-putting he must have been. He was on his way to a meeting with the Roman Senate when he was stabbed 23 times by a group of senators.[202]

Similarly, we remember the Romans positively as we admire their advances in the arts, government, and public works such as roads and aqueducts. Perhaps their greatest civil engineering project was the Roman Colosseum. It is on a par with the pyramids of Egypt. But what G-d sees is what went on inside the Colosseum. A couple thousand years have obscured our clarity regarding the unspeakable horror that was perpetrated against myriads of victims in the Colosseum. There is no video of what took place, so it is hard for us to appreciate how awful it was.

Almost everyone was complicit in the crimes against humanity that took place in the Colosseum. The Roman civilians who worked there stand guilty. Whether they were janitors, lion keepers, ticket takers, or managers, they were

---

[202] Robert Payne, *Ancient Rome* (New York, NY: ibooks, 2007)124.

wrong to participate in this evil by working there. The Roman citizens who attended the events and cheered the carnage stand guilty. Certainly, the Roman soldiers who applied force as needed to deliver the victims onto the Colosseum floor stand guilty. For not just criminals, but even innocent Christians were thrust onto the Colosseum floor and made to undergo a hellish end to their lives.[203]

There was one more who was present in the Colosseum. G-d was there, but He was not complicit. He saw it all, and He wept. G-d has given us the gifts of life and free will. Free will requires that we have the ability to do good or to sin. It was the Romans who sinned, not G-d. But He will not allow this sin to continue forever. One day, He will put an end to it. This is the message of the book of Daniel.

Eventually, Daniel grew old in captivity. One day he was reading in the book of Jeremiah where it was written that the Jews would be cast into exile for seventy years.[204] Daniel started calculating, and he realized that the seventy years were almost up! So what did he do? He prayed. Specifically, he confessed the great sin of the Jewish people in a lengthy and heartfelt prayer. This prayer is recorded in chapter 9, verses 4 through 19. Here is an excerpt from this prayer:

> "Open shame belongs to us, O L-rd, to our
> kings, our princes, and our fathers, because
> we have sinned against Thee. To the L-rd our

---

[203] Similarly, a great number of Jews were subject to being fed to wild beasts as well as being made to fight each other to the death for the sake of putting on a series of shows in multiple cities in Judea and Syria. The Jews subject to this gruesome fate were actually the survivors of the 70 CE siege who were being led away to become slaves following the defeat of Jerusalem. Josephus records these events in *Wars* 7.2.1 (23-24); 7.3.1 (37-40); and 7.5.1 (96).

[204] Jer. 25:11-12; 29:10.

G-d belong compassion and forgiveness, for we have rebelled against Him; nor have we obeyed the voice of the L-rd our G-d, to walk in His teachings which He set before us through His servants the prophets. Indeed all Israel has transgressed Thy law and turned aside, not obeying Thy voice; so the curse has been poured out on us, . . ."[205]

He used strong language to confess the sins of the nation, and his own sins as well.[206] He prayed with such language because the sins of the Jewish people were great. Then he beseeched G-d to fulfill His covenantal promises and allow them to return to their land and rebuild the Temple. To Daniel, it was astonishing that G-d could be so forgiving that He would give the Jews a second chance after all they had done. What mattered to Daniel was that G-d's plan in history be allowed to move forward. This required that the Jews be set free and return to their land to act as G-d's representatives again. In Daniel's words:

"O my G-d, incline Thine ear and hear! Open Thine eyes and see our desolations and the city which is called by Thy name; for we are not presenting our supplications before Thee on account of any merits of our own, but on account of Thy great compassion. O L-rd, hear! O L-rd forgive! O L-rd listen and take action! For Thine own sake, O my G-d, do not delay, because Thy city and Thy people are called by Thy name."[207]

---

[205] Dan. 9:8-11.
[206] Dan. 9:20.
[207] Dan. 9:18-19.

Upon uttering these words, the angel Gabriel appeared to him and gave him a new prophecy. This prophecy foretold the future of the Jews from that point on, and it is concise. It is given in four verses:

> "Seventy weeks have been decreed for your people and your holy city, to finish the transgression, to make an end of sin, to make atonement for iniquity, to bring in ever-lasting righteousness, to seal up vision and prophecy, and to anoint the most holy place. So you are to know and discern that from the issuing of a decree to restore and rebuild Jerusalem until Messiah the Prince there will be seven weeks and sixty-two weeks; it will be built again, with plaza and moat, even in times of distress. Then after the sixty-two weeks the Messiah will be cut off and have nothing, and the people of the prince who is to come will destroy the city and the sanctuary. And its end will come with a flood; even to the end there will be war; desolations are determined. And he will make a firm covenant with the many for one week, but in the middle of the week he will put a stop to sacrifice and grain offering; and on the wing of abominations will come one who makes desolate, even until a complete destruction, one that is decreed, is poured out on the one who makes desolate."[208]

In verse 24, the Hebrew word for weeks is "shābûa'." "Shābûa'" is like our English word "dozen." It does not strictly

---

[208] Dan. 9:24-27.

mean a set of seven days, but rather a set of seven somethings. The identity of the somethings is determined either by the word following "shābûa'" or by the context. In this case, the context has to do with the Jews' history of violating the sabbath year law.[209] In other words, the context deals with sets of seven years. So the seventy weeks that Daniel prophesied represent a period of seventy sets of seven years, or in other words, 490 years.

This 490-year period was to begin with a decree for the Jews to restore and rebuild Jerusalem. This is right in line with Daniel's prayer in the first twenty verses. G-d would work again with the Jews, and they would return to their land and rebuild Jerusalem.

Following the seventy-year period in which the Jews were in exile, there were multiple decrees given for the Jews to return to their land, including the first one given by King Cyrus at the end of the seventy-year period.[210] But only one of them matched this prophecy. That is the decree given by King Artaxerxes I of Persia in Nehemiah chapter 2. Nehemiah was the king's cupbearer, and when the king noticed that he was sad, Nehemiah told him why: the city of his ancestors' tombs was desolate and the city gates were destroyed by fire. Then Nehemiah asked him for permission to go to Jerusalem and rebuild it. Nehemiah even requested a decree from the king to rebuild the city wall of Jerusalem.[211] This would be a highly unusual request to be granted because it would enable the

---

[209] The context of Daniel chapter 9 encompasses sets of seven years based on 2 Chron. 36:20-21 and Jeremiah 25:11-12 and 29:10 in which the farmland of Israel had missed 70 Sabbath rest years. This means that for 490 years prior to the Babylonian exile, the Jews had not honored the Sabbath year law and given the land its rest. Thus, the context of Daniel 9 features sets of 7 years.

[210] 2 Chron. 36:22-23.

[211] Neh. 2:8.

Jews to defend themselves against the Persians if a conflict arose. But G-d was with Nehemiah, and Artaxerxes granted all of his requests. This happened in the twentieth year of his reign.[212] The dates of Artaxerxes' reign are known to historians, and the twentieth year of his reign took place in either 445 or 444 BCE.

Daniel was given this prophecy approximately one hundred years prior to the start date. Thus, the prophecy states that G-d would formally work with the Jews as His people to fully accomplish His plan for mankind over a period of 490 years starting in the year 445 or 444 BCE. Further, Daniel breaks this 490-year-long period into three sub-periods: a 49-year period, a 434-year period, and a final seven-year period. In addition, the final seven-year period is divided into two equal halves.

Setting aside the final seven-year period for the moment, 483 years following the start date would place you at either 39 or 40 CE. However, there was no year zero. In other words, the year following 1 BCE was 1 CE. Therefore, 483 years following 444 BCE is not 39 CE, but rather 40 CE. Nothing happened in either 40 or 41 CE that would make sense of this prophecy. However, Christian theologians have noted that in ancient Israel, and in the Hebrew Bible,[213] the Jewish calendar consisted of 12 months of 30 days comprising a 360-day year. Of course, years are actually 365.25 days long. Therefore, multiplying 483 times 360 and then dividing by 365.25 converts the 483 Biblical years into 476 calendar years. 476 years following the start date places you in the early 30s CE,

---

[212] Neh. 2:1, 8.

[213] In Genesis 7:11 and 8:4, a five-month period is delineated, and in Gen. 7:24 and 8:3, it is declared to be 150 days long; Josh McDowell, *Evidence that Demands a Verdict*, Revised Edition, (San Bernardino: HERE'S LIFE PUBLISHERS, INC., 1972, 1979) 172.

either 32 or 33 CE. This is the time of Jesus' crucifixion, and this is exactly what verse 26 predicted: "Then after the sixty-two weeks the Messiah will be cut off and have nothing, . . ."

G-d predicting the timing of the Messiah dying also makes sense in light of verse 24. One of the six outcomes G-d would perform through the Jewish people was to "make atonement for iniquity." Of course, the Jewish people are not capable of accomplishing this goal. As G-d made clear through the rituals that were performed on the Day of Atonement, no human is worthy to come before G-d, not even the high priest. Daniel, too, was unworthy to come before G-d, and he was an extremely godly man. In fact, none of Daniel's sins are recorded in the Hebrew Bible. They are for Moses and David, but not for Daniel. Only acts of extreme faith towards G-d are recorded for Daniel. When he prayed, angels were dispatched. For as Gabriel stated, Daniel was "highly esteemed."[214] And yet, Daniel was human, and in chapter 9 verse 20, he confessed his sins to G-d. Thus, he prayed for G-d to deliver the Jews not because of their merit, but only on the basis of His grace and mercy.[215]

So how could G-d use His people to make atonement for iniquity? After all, they could not make atonement for themselves, let alone in any global sense for the sake of mankind. Only G-d can provide atonement. But He could use the Jews to help with this great work if He came down from heaven and was born a Jew.

* * * * *

When the Jews returned from Babylonia, they rebuilt the Temple. There they performed the rituals prescribed in the Law. In addition, the Jews were faithful to never again violate

---

[214] Dan. 9:23.
[215] Dan. 9:19.

the first two commandments and bow before idols. These were difficult days. The Jews were an occupied people; first by the Persians, then the Greeks, and then the Romans. They were only independent for an approximately 75-year long period in the second half of the Greek Empire. Some of the foreign rulers were bearable, and some were not. In particular, the Greek ruler Antiochus Epiphanes IV was an evil man who clamped down on the Jews and even blasphemed G-d. He compelled the Jews to suspend virtually all of their religious practices and instead worship Zeus (and in essence him as he viewed himself to be a manifestation of Zeus).[216] He even went so far as to erect an altar on top of the altar of burnt offering and sacrifice a pig on it. This took place in December 167 BCE.[217] So heinous would this man be that Daniel recorded very detailed prophecies of his deeds in Daniel 8:9-14, 23-25, and 11:21-35. Needless to say, faithful Jews did not submit to this godless man's orders, even at the cost of their own lives. The most famous Jewish historical event of the 483-year period was the righteous Jewish rebellion to this man's authority, the Maccabean Revolt. G-d was with the Maccabees family and all the brave Jews who stood with them. Daniel predicted the result of their revolt when he wrote that the "holy place will be properly restored."[218] Of course, these events are still celebrated today on the Jewish holiday of Chanukah.

However, as consequential and evil as Antiochus Epiphanes was, Daniel also prophesied of another who will arise in the final seven years of history. Antiochus is a type of

---

[216] F. F. Bruce, *Israel and the Nations* (Grand Rapids: William B. Eerdmans Publishing Company, 1969, 1985) 145.

[217] Walvoord and Zuck, eds., *The Bible Knowledge Commentary*, Old Testament 1370.

[218] Dan. 8:14.

him. This other man will be like Antiochus, but he will cause far more damage. In the Christian New Testament, this man is called the Antichrist. He will be energized by Satan, and he too will blaspheme G-d in the Temple. He is the "prince who is to come" in verse 26, and his interactions with the Jews are depicted in verse 27. There is much prophecy in Daniel about this man as well, and you can tell which evil ruler is being predicted in each prophecy as Antiochus comes out of the Greek Empire, but the Antichrist comes out of the Roman Empire. Prophecies about the Antichrist are given in Daniel 7:7-11, 19-26; 9:26-27; and 11:36-45.

In verse 26, it says that the people of the prince who is to come would destroy Jerusalem and the Temple. Thus, the prince who is to come, or Antichrist, will be a Roman emperor as it was the Romans who destroyed Jerusalem and the Temple in 70 CE. That being so, in this verse we have a prophetic time gap. It is subtle, but look at the verb tense: "the people of the prince who is to come will destroy the city . . ." So the prince will come later, but his people will destroy the city now. This Roman prince will be a prominent player in the final seven-year period in which G-d will work with the Jewish people. Furthermore, we know from Daniel 11:40 that this man will take part in a great war that will occur at "the end time." Thus, in chapter 9, Daniel was predicting that G-d would work again with the Jews, who at that time were standing on the sidelines in Babylonia. Specifically, He would work with them for 490 years, but there would be a gap following the death of the Messiah until the final seven-year period which will occur at the very end of history.

That there would be a gap in the history of the Roman Empire is also implied in the prophecy in Daniel chapter 2 where the Roman Empire is represented by the legs and feet of the statue. The two different body parts, the legs and the feet, represent two different stages of this empire. Further, whereas the legs are made of iron, and sure enough, the Roman Empire was as strong as iron, the feet will be made of a composite of iron and clay.[219] In other words, there will be a compositional change that will take place in the second stage of the empire. So, whereas the Roman Empire emerged from the city of Rome and the surrounding region in ancient Italy, perhaps, the second stage of the Roman Empire will emerge from an alliance between the Italians and another people or multiple other peoples. Also, this second stage may not be as strong as the Roman Empire was in its heyday. But rather, it may have brittle parts which, like clay pottery, can easily be broken into pieces by a competent enemy. In addition, in the next verse in chapter 2, it says that a great stone will strike the statue on the feet.[220] That is because the feet represent the empire that will be in place at the end of time when the Messiah comes and puts a stop to Gentile kingdoms forever.[221] The other empires will already long since have vanished from the stage of history including the legs which represent the original Roman Empire. But the point is that there will be a connection between the final empire and the Roman Empire. The final one will be a revived version of the Roman Empire, albeit it will be different in some fashion.

It is notable that G-d was taking a break from working with the Jews during the Babylonian exile. He was disciplining them for their centuries of sin and disregard for His Law. The Jews suffered greatly at the outset of this event as recorded in the book of Lamentations in which Jerusalem was under siege and there was starvation and even

---

[219] Dan. 2:33.

[220] Dan. 2:34.

[221] Dennis McCallum, Bible, teaching, "Nebuchadnezzar's Dream (Dan. 2:1-47)," 7/9/2017, https://teachings.dwellcc.org/teaching/1037 (accessed May 5, 2022).

cannibalism. Then Jerusalem and the Temple were burned to the ground and the survivors were hauled off as captives. So too, according to Daniel, in either 32 or 33 CE, G-d would again take a break from working with the Jews. Further, Daniel predicted that Jerusalem would again be destroyed, including the Temple. Indeed, the Roman assault on Jerusalem in 70 CE turned out to be a carbon copy of the Babylonian conquest of Jerusalem. There was a siege in which the people starved to death and resorted to cannibalism. The siege was followed by great bloodshed when the Roman soldiers breeched the wall. Then the city and the Temple were destroyed and the survivors were hauled off into captivity. Only, this time the Jews were not being disciplined for their idolatry or failure to pay heed to the Law, but rather because of their participation in the "cutting off" of the Messiah. In the words of John the disciple, "He was in the world, and the world was made through Him, and the world did not know Him. He came to His own, and those who were His own did not receive Him."[222] Surely, Jesus was rejected by the Jewish people. In this case, the siege and fall of Jerusalem took place a little less than forty years after Jesus was crucified. Nonetheless, according to Daniel, G-d was not working with the Jewish people during the intervening years. But rather, they were on their own.

Returning to verse 26, it also says that there would be periods of desolation in Jerusalem following the Roman assault. Daniel was right again as surely there have been periods of desolation over the last two thousand years. Of course, this only makes sense as G-d's people have been in exile. Daniel also used the Hebrew word that is translated as "desolations" in this verse, in another verse. Not surprisingly,

---

[222] Jn. 1:11-12.

he used it in verse 18 to describe the state of Jerusalem in his day when the Jews were in exile in Babylonia.

Just as the Jews have become a nation again in the land of Israel after all these years, we can also expect that the Roman Empire will be revived at the end of human history. In addition, Daniel predicted that the Temple will be rebuilt at the end of time. He predicted this in verse 27 where it says: ". . . but in the middle of the week he will put a stop to sacrifice and grain offering; and on the wing of abominations will come one who makes desolate." This is exactly what the Antichrist's forerunner, Antiochus Epiphanes, did when he desecrated the Temple.[223] Therefore, we can expect the Temple to be rebuilt, for the Antichrist will desecrate it in the middle of the final seven years of history.

* * * * *

A question that may be asked is: why did Daniel prophesy of a 490-year period consisting of three parts as opposed to two? In other words, why does he delineate the 49-year period from the 434-year period that follows it? Unfortunately, the answer to that question is not clear. Perhaps archaeologists and historians will one day discover a significant event that took place in Israel 49 years after Artaxerxes issued his decree.

* * * * *

What an amazing chapter Daniel 9 is. In this chapter, G-d backs up His claim that only He can see the future with an array of very specific and unlikely prophecies. In the scant four verse set beginning in verse 24, which was written during the 500s BCE, Daniel lays out a framework for the rest of

---

[223] Dan. 11:31.

Jewish history. This framework includes the following elements:

1. a tremendous list of six outcomes that G-d will accomplish through the Jewish people and their Messiah

2. the length of time that G-d would work with the Jews

3. the date when He would restart working with the Jews which coincided with a decree to restore and rebuild Jerusalem

4. the date of the death of the Messiah

5. the destruction of Jerusalem and the Temple by the Romans after the 483-year period

6. periods of desolation in Jerusalem following its destruction by the Romans

7. information about the final seven-year period in which G-d will work with the Jews

   a. it will take place an indeterminate amount of time after the Messiah is killed

   b. it will take place at the end of human history

   c. a new arrogant man will arise who will seek to rule the world

   d. he will lead a revived Roman Empire

   e. he will make a covenant with the Jews at the beginning of the seven years

   f. in the middle of the seven years, he will break the covenant, suspend Jewish religious practices, and desecrate the Temple like Antiochus Epiphanes IV did during the Greek Empire

   g. at the end of the seven years, G-d will bring destruction crashing down on this man

8. a new reality characterized by "everlasting righteousness" that will take place after the final seven-year period

This framework lays the foundation for the rest of Biblical prophecy. The rest of Biblical prophecy, consisting of the end times prophecies found in both the Hebrew Bible and the Christian New Testament, fills in the details.

History has proceeded exactly as Daniel prophesied it would in items 3 through 6 above having already occurred. We now await the remaining items to come to pass at the end of history.

But Daniel chapter 9 is more than just an amazing series of prophecies; it also contains a message of G-d's love and mercy. One of the key events in G-d's plan entails the Messiah being put to death. This event is necessary to achieve the goal of making atonement for iniquity. The Messiah prophesied by Daniel has to be Jesus. Any attempt to claim that there was another Jewish Messiah who was killed in the early 30s CE defies credulity.[224] Yet, one may ask: how could G-d come to

---

[224] Rashi's interpretation of this prophecy is that the 490 years begins in 587/586 BCE with the destruction of Jerusalem and the Temple by the Babylonians and ends in 70 CE with the destruction of same by the Romans. Further, his interpretation is that there would be two Messiahs, and that in 70 CE, they wound up being King Agrippa and the High Priest. (*The Books of Daniel, Ezra, Nehemiah,* translation and commentary by Rabbi A. J. Rosenberg (Brooklyn: The Judaica Press, 1991, 2000) 86-90.) Rashi's basis for making this dual designation is because the literal translation of the word Messiah is the anointed one; and Agrippa and the High Priest were both in office at the time of the 70 CE Roman conquest. But Daniel does not predict that two Messiahs would be killed. As well, Agrippa was a friend to Rome who died 20 to 30 years after 70 CE. In addition, Agrippa was a typical self-serving king, and in no way can he be attributed with advancing or fulfilling any of the 6 godly outcomes given in verse 24. Nor does Rashi make the case that the High Priest contributed to any

earth and take on the form of a man? The answer is: G-d can do anything. He created the universe and life. He is certainly capable of coming to earth in the form of a man. Why would G-d do this? He did it because He loves us. In much the same way as many of the men on board the Titanic went into the water and gave up their lives so that their wives and children could have seats in the lifeboats, so too, G-d has sacrificed Himself to pay the price for our eternal souls. Simply put, G-d's love is astounding, and Jesus is a hero.

---

of these goals. Furthermore, three and a half years prior to the final defeat of Jerusalem in 70 CE, no abomination took place that in any way resembled the blasphemous acts committed by Antiochus Epiphanes IV. Also, Rashi does not explain how he winds up with the 490th year terminating in 70 CE, some 655 to 656 years after 587/586 BCE. In short, Rashi finds a way to bypass Jesus, but he does not do it through interpreting Daniel in a literal sense. In chapter 9, Daniel interprets Jeremiah's prophecy of a 70-year Babylonian exile literally; and then he delivers a prophecy that contains a specific number of years. Perhaps G-d is trying to tell us to interpret Daniel's prophecy the same way Daniel interpreted Jeremiah's prophecy, literally.

23

THE LIBERATING
MESSIAH

Throughout the first part of his life, Moses was not a confident man, but he stepped forward anyway to speak the words of G-d to the wicked Egyptian pharaoh. Pharaoh thought little of what Moses had to say. A conflict ensued, and G-d prevailed.

At the end of time, instead of just one vile king rebelling against G-d, there will be many. Yet, one of them will rise above the rest as he will outdo the others in deviousness and inhumaneness. He is the Antichrist, and he will lead the world into a state of hell. He will be satanically empowered, and there will be attesting miracles performed on his behalf, just as there were by the magicians for Pharaoh.

Further compounding the suffering at the end of time will be the giant leap in technology that has been made in the 3,500 years that have gone by since the days of Pharaoh. The Bible foretells that in the future, our technological advances will be used for evil. The pharaoh who was on the throne at the time of Moses' birth ordered the soldiers to throw Jewish baby boys in the Nile one at a time.[225] His eventual successor will aim guided missiles at hospitals and take out entire maternity wards with the push of a button. One may ask, how could Jewish suffering ever get worse considering what they have already been through? This is how.

Thus, referring to the end of time, Jeremiah wrote:

> Now these are the words which the L-rd spoke concerning Israel and concerning Judah, "For thus says the L-rd, 'I have heard a sound of terror, of dread, and there is no peace. Ask now, and see, if a male can give birth. Why do I see every man *with* his hands on his loins as a woman in childbirth? And *why* have all faces turned pale? Alas! for the day is great, there is none like it; and it is the time of Jacob's distress, but he will be saved from it. . ..'"[226]

This metaphor has long since gone out of use. It sounds unpleasant to our ears. But it is simply a figure of speech communicating that the last days will be so horrendous that it is unfathomable.

But praise G-d, for just at the right moment, He will send His Messiah to put an end to the Antichrist and the other tyrannical world rulers. He will prevail and He will regather the Jews to their homeland.

Of course, at the end of time, not only the Jews, but everyone will be suffering. War and destruction will be taking place all over the world. This will be the final war, and nuclear

---

[225] Ex. 1:22.
[226] Jer. 30:4-7.

weapons will be used. In fact, they will be used liberally. In the words of Isaiah:

> The earth is broken asunder, the earth is split through, the earth is shaken violently. The earth reels to and from like a drunkard, and it totters like a shack, for its transgression is heavy upon it, and it will fall, never to rise again. So it will happen in that day, that the L-rd will punish the host of heaven, on high, and the kings of the earth, on earth.[227]

Jesus put it this way:

> ". . . for then there will be a great tribulation, such as has not occurred since the beginning of the world until now, nor ever shall. And unless those days had been cut short, no life would have been saved; but for the sake of the elect those days shall be cut short."[228]

Nuclear weapons will be launched to such an extent that life on earth will be in jeopardy. It appears that the Messiah will come at the very moment when all the missiles are in the air crisscrossing the globe, and He will put a stop to it. After all, the earth belongs to G-d. It is merely on loan to us. And so will end the days of human self-rule.

Needless to say, there is a great amount of prophecy about the final war and the last battle in the Hebrew Bible. Here are

---

[227] Isa. 24:19-21.
[228] Mt. 24:21-22.

a couple examples of these prophecies; the first one is Psalm 2, and the second one is a part of Ezekiel 39:

> Why are the nations in an uproar, and the peoples devising a vain thing? The kings of the earth take their stand, and the rulers take counsel together against the L-rd and against His Anointed. "Let us tear their fetters apart, and cast away their cords from us!"
>
> He who sits in the heavens laughs, the L-rd scoffs at them. Then He will speak to them in His anger and terrify them in His fury: "But as for Me, I have installed My King upon Zion, My holy mountain. I will surely tell of the decree of the L-rd: He said to Me, 'Thou art My Son, today I have begotten Thee. Ask of Me, and I will surely give the nations as Thine inheritance, and the very ends of the earth as Thy possession. Thou shalt break them with a rod of iron, Thou shalt shatter them like earthenware.'"
>
> Now therefore, O kings, show discernment; take warning, O judges of the earth. Worship the L-rd with reverence, and rejoice with trembling. Do homage to the Son, lest He become angry, and you perish in the way, for His wrath may soon be kindled. How blessed are all who take refuge in Him!

and,

> "And you, son of man, prophesy against Gog, and say, 'Thus says the L-rd G-d, "Behold, I am against you, O Gog, prince of Rosh, Meshech, and Tubal; and I shall turn you

around, drive you on, take you up from the remotest parts of the north, and bring you against the mountains of Israel. And I shall strike your bow from your left hand, and dash down your arrows from your right hand. You shall fall on the mountains of Israel, you and all your troops, and the peoples who are with you; I shall give you as food to every kind of predatory bird and beast of the field. You will fall on the open field; for it is I who have spoken," declares the L-rd G-d. "And I shall send fire upon Magog and those who inhabit the coastlands in safety; and they will know that I am the L-rd.

And My holy name I shall make known in the midst of My people Israel; and I shall not let My holy name be profaned anymore. And the nations will know that I am the L-rd, the Holy One in Israel. Behold, it is coming and it shall be done," declares the L-rd G-d. "That is the day of which I have spoken. . .."""[229]

In Psalm 2, we see the Messiah shattering the Gentile nations. This is going to take place when the Gentile world comes together in an attempt to overthrow G-d. How insane. In fact, this suicidal plot by the Gentiles will arise out of a state of deception. There are a lot of lies permeating society about G-d's character, and these leaders and their peoples will believe them all. Astonishingly, even still, G-d's desire is for their good. That is why this psalm was written. It is a warning to them to wake up, turn to G-d, and receive His offer of forgiveness and reconciliation. For there will come a time

---

[229] Ezek. 39:1-8.

when it will be too late to turn back to G-d. G-d is extremely patient, and He is waiting. He is giving people as much time as possible to accept His offer of salvation. But eventually, He will not be able to wait any longer. Otherwise, all life will be destroyed.

The prophecy from Ezekiel deals with a contingency of nations or peoples from northern Eurasia. These peoples will be opposed to Israel and will send their armies to launch an assault on the Jewish state. The names of the peoples given in this passage are the ancient names of the peoples who make up the country of Russia today. This makes sense as Ezekiel tells us that these nations are from "the remotest parts of the north." For that is where Russia is located, as far north as you can get from Israel. Indeed, Moscow is located almost directly north of Israel. Interestingly, Russia has been a major destabilizing influence in the world throughout the twentieth and twenty-first centuries. Furthermore, the Russians have been enemies of modern-day Israel. Thus, this ancient prophecy fits right in line with the geopolitical setting of today.

There are also other prophecies about peoples from other lands who will come to Israel to do harm to the Jews.[230] In fact, there are so many end time prophecies that we cannot cover them all in this book. The prophecy from Ezekiel 39 is a good example of these prophecies that foretell the hostility the Gentiles will exhibit towards the Jews at the end of history. At the very end, there will be a final battle in which armies from all over the world will come together to attack G-d's people.[231] But as opposed to the ancient invasions by the Babylonians and the Romans, which succeeded, this time the Gentile

---

[230] Ezek. 38:1-16.
[231] Zech. 12:2-3.

invasion will fail. For G-d will act on behalf of the Jews, and all the Gentile soldiers will die in Israel.

The Messiah will come, and He will put down the Gentile rebellion and establish justice. G-d is righteous, and justice will not be compromised for any sin that has ever been committed.

The book of Nahum is an example of G-d executing justice. In that case, it was the Assyrians who had been so wicked for so long that they forfeited the right to exist any longer. Like the Romans who would come later, they were heartless, and they committed grotesque crimes against humanity. In addition, they fully embraced the sinful worship practices and beliefs of paganism. Here is Nahum's prophecy of their downfall:

> She is emptied! Yes, she is desolate and waste! Hearts are melting and knees knocking! Also anguish is in the whole body, and all their faces are grown pale! Where is the den of the lions and the feeding place of the young lions, where the lion, lioness, and lion's cub prowled, with nothing to disturb *them*? The lion tore enough for his cubs, killed *enough* for his lionesses, and filled his lairs with prey and his dens with torn flesh. "Behold, I am against you," declares the L-rd of hosts. "I will burn up her chariots in smoke, a sword will devour your young lions, I will cut off your prey from the land, and no longer will the voice of your messengers be heard."
>
> Woe to the bloody city, completely full of lies *and* pillage; *her* prey never departs. The noise of the whip, the noise of the rattling of the wheel, galloping horses, and bounding

chariots! Horsemen charging, swords flashing, spears gleaming, many slain, a mass of corpses, and countless dead bodies—they stumble over the dead bodies! *All* because of the many harlotries of the harlot, the charming one, the mistress of sorceries, who sells nations by her harlotries and families by her sorceries. "Behold, I am against you," declares the L-rd of hosts, "And I will lift up your skirts over your face, and show to the nations your nakedness and to the kingdoms your disgrace. I will throw filth on you and make you vile, and set you up as a spectacle. And it will come about that all who see you will shrink from you and say, 'Nineveh is devastated! Who will grieve for her?' Where will I seek comforters for you?"[232]

What a shocking passage this is. It is hard to believe this is in the Hebrew Bible, but it is. The sin of man is so disgusting that the justice it requires cannot be sanitized. The Assyrians were the lions of the jungle in the ancient world. They viewed all the other nations as their prey. They killed and they took, and they did it barbarically. When they defeated Thebes, they took all the small children and "dashed them to pieces."[233] They performed this insane act on each street so the people could see children they personally knew suffer this brutal fate. Winning the battle was not good enough for the Assyrians. They had to go further.

Finally, they went too far. G-d waited until the last possible moment for them to change their hearts, but

---

[232] Nah. 2:10 (11) - 3:7.
[233] Nah. 3:10.

eventually the Assyrians' sins were so grievous and so many that He could not allow them to perpetrate any more violence. It was time for justice to be served. It was their turn to experience soldiers storming through their capital and to suffer massive numbers of deaths such that their streets were littered with corpses.

In terms of the unseemly metaphor in the passage from Nahum, the harlot is Nineveh, the capital of Assyria. It was there where the lies were conceived, the wars of aggression were sanctioned, and the plunder was collected. Nineveh was also a center for paganism and the occult. Needless to say, there were no prophecies coming from their "gods." That is not to say that the devotees did not have a religious experience, because they did. Indeed, they were contacting the spiritual world. The problem is that they were contacting the forces of darkness in the heavenly places. There are certain doors in this life that you should never open, for if you do, you can become ensnared by evil. Engaging in the degrading and sinful worship practices of paganism is one of those doors. The Assyrians were devout worshippers of a pantheon of debauched pagan deities. Needless to say, this contributed to their lust for military conquest and their utter lack of respect for human life.

So Nahum foretold that the day would come when G-d would put an end to this city and expose the hidden secrets of its people. What the surrounding nations already knew about the Assyrians was disgusting. What the Assyrians felt the need to hide must have been unimaginable. But it was time for justice, and it was time for their shame to be revealed. No doubt, G-d wanted to use their judgement to warn the rest of the world what will happen to you if you cast Him aside and give yourself over to sin.

So too, the Messiah will execute justice and deliver the Jews from Gentile aggression when He comes at the end of the age. Then He will establish a state of peace like nothing the world has ever seen before:

> And He will judge between the nations, and will render decisions for many peoples; and they will hammer their swords into plowshares, and their spears into pruning hooks. Nation will not lift up sword against nation, and never again will they learn war.[234]

Isn't it true that there has never really been peace? Throughout history, there has either been war or essentially a cease-fire period which aggressor nations utilized to re-arm for the next war. But when the Messiah comes, that will all be over!

Of course, when Jesus came the first time, two thousand years ago, this was not the outcome. Two thousand years ago the Jews were an occupied people. In fact, the Jews had been an occupied people for nearly all of the 570-year period in which they were back in their land prior to Jesus' arrival. First, the Persians were their rulers, then the Greeks, and finally the Romans. Surely, the Gentiles mistreated the Jews and disrespected G-d. The Romans went so far as to desecrate the Holy City with pagan effigies.[235] It only makes sense that the Jews would look to the prophets and place their hope in the predictions of the Messiah and this wondrous day when Gentile offenses will cease forever. It would have been easy for the Jews to overlook the parts of the double-reference prophecies referring to the Messiah coming in humility to pay the price for the sins of men. After all, it was not very clear how these parts meshed with the references to the Messiah coming in power to deliver the Jews. When Jesus showed up,

---

[234] Isa. 2:4.
[235] Josephus, *Antiquities* 18.3.1 (55).

He performed miracles and taught spiritual truth, but He also treated the Romans He encountered with kindness. Hence, the Jewish people were not sure what to make of Him. After all, He certainly was not crushing the Roman army and setting the Jews free. The religious leaders concluded that He was not the Messiah. What the Jews did not understand was that the Messiah has a two-part mission and that Jesus was only fulfilling the first part of His mission at that time. The Jewish people should have studied the messianic prophecies and prayed for understanding regarding the seeming incongruity between the two parts of the Messiah's mission. But it appears that most of the Jews did not do that as there was a rush to judgement and they rejected Jesus.

In fact, even Jesus' disciples were confused about this matter. It was not until after He resurrected and re-explained it to them that they finally understood that there are two comings of the Messiah.

G-d is not like us. Sometimes our thinking is clouded by our innate defensiveness. G-d is the author of life, and He knows us better than we know ourselves. He has always seen the Jews' predicament clearly. He knows that just as the Gentiles pose a clear and present danger to the Jews in this life, so too the Jews' sins pose a threat to them in the next life. Hence, there have always been two parts to G-d's plan. Jesus had to come the first time to liberate people from having to pay the price of justice for their sins. He will come back to liberate the Jews from oppression and violence.

A fair question to ask is, why is the time gap so long between the two comings? After all, it has been almost two thousand years since Jesus came. Here are two answers:

1. G-d does not act to execute justice until it is fully warranted. No one will ever be able to claim they could

have turned things around if G-d had only given them more time. Indeed, all will stand guilty, and their mouths will be shut when they appear before the judgement seat of G-d.

The Amorites were an exceedingly sinful people. They are another example of a people who were so evil that they forfeited the right to exist on earth. Nonetheless, G-d would not cut their stay short by even a minute as He waited until they reached a point of utter depravity. Once they did, He gave their land to the Jews. But He waited four long centuries to bring down His judgement, even though His people were suffering greatly as slaves in Egypt.[236]

So too at the end of time, G-d will wait until mankind has completely forfeited the right to rule itself before Jesus returns.

2. G-d has been at work hard during this period between the two comings of the Messiah to reach people throughout the earth. Of all things, He seeks a relationship with Gentiles as Jesus paid the price for our sins as well. Surely the Jews are G-d's people, but it was always His intention to provide salvation to all people. Hence, the closing line of His covenantal promise to Abraham was: "And in you all the families of the earth shall be blessed."[237] G-d's promises to Abraham started with he and his wife having a child. Ultimately, their family would grow into a nation. In addition, there would one day come a special individual from Abraham and Sarah's descendants, the Messiah. It is this special one whom G-d would use to bless all the families of the earth.

---

[236] Gen. 15:13, 16.
[237] Gen. 12:3b.

Just before Jesus ascended into heaven, His disciples asked Him when He was going to return to fulfill the rest of the works of the Messiah. He replied:

"It is not for you to know times or epochs which the Father has fixed by His own authority; but you shall receive power when the Holy Spirit has come upon you; and you shall be My witnesses both in Jerusalem, and in all Judea and Samaria, and even to the remotest part of the earth."[238]

G-d was not ready at that point to reveal the length of time before Jesus' return. However, it appears clear that it would be quite some time as He commissioned His followers to take the message of G-d's offer of salvation to the entire world, and that is no small feat. Indeed, Jesus' desire is for all people to be reconciled to G-d through His sacrifice on the cross.

Jesus' disciple Peter confirmed that this process would take an indeterminate but very long amount of time. Indeed, Peter wrote that it would take so long that eventually people would make fun of Christians who will persevere in claiming that Jesus will return:

"Know this first of all, that in the last days mockers will come with *their* mocking, following after their own lusts, and saying, "Where is the promise of His coming? For ever since the fathers fell asleep, all continues just as it was from the beginning of creation."

. . .

---

[238] Acts 1:7-8.

But do not let this one *fact* escape your notice, beloved, that with the L-rd one day is as a thousand years, and a thousand years as one day. The L-rd is not slow about His promise, as some count slowness, but is patient toward you, not wishing for any to perish but for all to come to repentance."[239]

Praise G-d. He loves all people, and He is at work to reach every person who will turn to Him. Furthermore, He will not rush or curtail that effort prematurely even though His people have been suffering greatly for a very long time.

There is a parallel passage in Genesis 18 and 19 in which G-d judges the ancient city of Sodom. It is emphasized in that passage that G-d would not destroy the city until every innocent person was removed first. And so it will be at the end of time. G-d will not bring the curtain down on history until every person who is willing to receive salvation is reached first.

Yet, one day the end of history will arrive. For just as the day finally came when Moses delivered the Jews from slavery in Egypt, and just as the day finally came when Nineveh fell, so too this day will come. For G d can see the future, and all of the prophecies pertaining to the end of time will come to pass. Furthermore, G d is faithful, and He will fulfill every promise He made to Abraham and the Jews. Surely, it has been a long, hard road, but one day Jesus will return and deliver the Jews from Gentile tyranny forever.

---

[239] 2 Pet. 3:3-4, 8-9.

24

ZECHARIAH 12:10

Zechariah is one of the last three prophetic books written in the Hebrew Bible. It was written around the same time as the book of Haggai. The historic setting consisted of the Jewish people returning from exile in Babylonia and encountering obstacles as they were trying to rebuild the Temple. Haggai's book dealt with these circumstances. But the book of Zechariah does not. Rather, Zechariah used the historic events of the return from Babylonia and the rebuilding of Solomon's Temple as a springboard to prophesy about a future return from exile and rebuilding of the Temple at the end of history. In addition, G-d used Zechariah to examine the sinfulness of man in juxtaposition to G-d's attributes of justice, faithfulness, and compassion.

Here is an example of a passage from Zechariah that we can deduce is not about Zechariah's day and their efforts at that time to rebuild the Temple. But rather, it is about the far distant future:

> ". . . 'Therefore, thus says the L-rd, "I will return to Jerusalem with compassion; My house will be built in it," declares the L-rd of hosts, "and a measuring line will be stretched over Jerusalem."'. . . Again, proclaim saying, 'Thus says the L-rd of hosts, "My cities will again overflow with prosperity, and the L-rd will again comfort Zion and again choose Jerusalem.""[240]

In this passage, the angel of the L-rd is speaking of a time when G-d will again comfort Zion and bless the cities of Judah. In the second verse above, the word "again" is used four times in a single sentence. In other words, the speaker was not referring to the present return from exile in which the Jews met with difficulty when they came back from Babylonia. But rather, the angel of the L-rd was speaking of another return that would take place in the future in which the returnees would meet with great ease and G-d's blessing. This interpretation is confirmed by the content in the remainder of the book in which there is prophecy of a battle of apocalyptic proportions followed by a state of global peace and a time of blessing for the Jews. The peace will be maintained by the Messiah who will rule from Jerusalem. Needless to say, nothing remotely resembling this prediction occurred following the return of the Jews from Babylonia. Indeed, they would go on to be an occupied territory until their re-expulsion from the land in 70 CE.

Zechariah records a series of very symbolic visions in the first five and a half chapters. It is not clear what is being

---

[240] Zech. 1:16-17.

prophesied in these passages. However, these visions do contain clues that tie them to other prophecies in the Hebrew Bible as well as to passages in the book of Revelation. In this way, they fit into the mosaic of Biblical prophecy. From the middle of Zechariah chapter 6 to the end of the book, Zechariah writes in a more standard Biblical prophetic script. But these prophecies are still somewhat ambiguous as they utilize literary devices and lack details.

Have you ever done a 500-piece jigsaw puzzle? Some of the pieces are edge pieces, some pieces have a very identifiable image such as a letter that you can easily match with the photo on the box, and some are blurry and hard to identify. Typically, you do the edge pieces and the ones with identifiable images first. Then you may separate out the light blue pieces into a group for when it is time to do the sky. You may also separate the pieces into groups based on their shapes as only certain shaped pieces will fit into certain spots. But in terms of the blurry pieces, they are a mystery and typically they get done last. Once you fit the last piece into place and complete the puzzle, it all comes into focus. A number of the passages in Zechariah are the blurry pieces of Biblical prophecy.

Another characteristic we see in the writing in the book of Zechariah is that it is shocking. Some of the verses slap you in the face in an attempt to wake you up and make you think. Here are three examples:

1. And I took my staff, Favor, and cut it in pieces, to break my covenant which I had made with all the peoples.[241]

---

[241] Zech. 11:10.

First of all, the phrase "all the peoples" sounds like a reference to the Gentiles. But the word that is translated as "peoples" can be translated simply as "people" since that is still a plural noun. [242] If that is the case, then Zechariah is referring to the Jewish people. This interpretation fits the context and makes sense. Thus, it appears that Zechariah was trying to shock his audience in this verse. For he wrote that G-d would break a covenant, and His favor for the Jews would be shattered. In this word picture, G-d is the Shepherd of the Jews. But something would happen and G-d would not be pleased with the Jewish people. Therefore, He would take His staff of favor and cut it into pieces. Having just returned from exile, this statement should have taken their breath away. The Jews should have fallen to their knees and sought G-d's will from their hearts. Tragically, they just plowed ahead.

Surely, this verse is an apt description of G-d's dealings with the Jews over the last two thousand years. In all the places the Jews were driven, they never forgot about G-d.[243] But He showed them no favor as they have been subjected to two thousand years of horrid antisemitism. The Europeans, the Arabs, the Russians under the Czars, the Russians under the Bolsheviks, the Catholics, the Protestants, and certainly the Nazis all stand guilty before G-d for their treatment of His people. They are all guilty of injustice, hatred, and violence. But one day, G-d will reestablish His people in their land forever. Indeed, He has already begun it!

It is interesting that prior to the Babylonian captivity, G-d sent a chorus of prophets over a period of centuries to warn

---

[242] Paul, L. Redditt, *Haggai, Zechariah, Malachi*, The New Century Bible Commentary. Gen.Eds. Ronald E. Clements, and Matthew Black, (Grand Rapids, Michigan: William B. Eerdmans Publishing Company, 1995) 125-126.

[243] Zech. 10:9.

the Jews to turn from their sin, lest they face the horrors of war culminating in banishment from their land. Indeed, well over a hundred chapters in the Hebrew Bible were written by the prophets warning the Jewish people of the coming calamity. But G-d did not similarly warn the Jews who returned from Babylonia that they, too, were in danger of judgement. As we know today, the returning Jews would eventually go on to face virtually the same judgment in 70 CE. The residents of Jerusalem endured a horrendous multiyear siege which culminated in a brief moment of horror when the soldiers broke down the wall and poured into the city. The final blow was again the banishment of the survivors.

The reasons given by the earlier prophets for their warnings were very clear, and the fate the Jews would suffer was spelled out in precise detail. The reasons for the earlier judgement consisted of, first and foremost, their worship of idols, followed by a litany of other sins. These sins included: businessmen cheating; judges accepting bribes; people offering sacrifices insincerely; leaders leading for their own benefit; and the entire nation turning a blind eye to the needs of the poor. Needless to say, the people grew weary of the prophets repeating the same warnings over and over again and they did not heed them.

Following their return from Babylonia, the Jewish people did learn an important lesson. They had become convinced that their G-d is the real G-d who judges. Therefore, they let go of worshipping idols. Nonetheless, the people still did not have a heart for G-d. They feared Him, but they did not honor and obey Him from their hearts like Daniel did. Neither did they relate to Him personally like David did. Of course, their attitude manifested itself in a variety of sins. But the root problem was their heart attitude.

Unlike the centuries leading up to the Babylonian exile, this time there were only a few passages warning the Jews that they needed to change. Zechariah chapter 11 is one of them. But this warning in Zechariah 11 is not like the warnings issued by Isaiah, Jeremiah, and others which were very clear. Rather, this warning is somewhat ambiguous. Nonetheless, chapter 11 was written to get the Jews' attention. In fact, the verse before the above verse is eye-catching as well: "Then I said, 'I will not pasture you. What is to die, let it die, and what is to be annihilated, let it be annihilated; and let those who are left eat one another's flesh.'"[244] The reference to cannibalism at the end of this verse would have caught the attention of the Zechariah's immediate audience, many of whom lived through the Babylonian siege. So Zechariah was trying to get them to wake up spiritually. But we humans are a stubborn lot. The Jews again disregarded these words from G-d. Tragically, their day of judgement would come and the grievous act of cannibalism would take place again in Jerusalem during the prolonged Roman siege.

Although Zechariah does not spell it out exactly, he nonetheless appears to give the reason for the coming judgment in the next few verses of chapter 11:

> And I said to them, "If it is good in your sight, give *me* my wages; but if not, never mind!" So they weighed out thirty *shekels* of silver as my wages. Then the L-rd said to me, "Throw it to the potter, *that* magnificent price at which I was valued by them." So I took the thirty *shekels* of silver and threw them to the potter in the house of the L-rd."[245]

This prophecy was fulfilled by Jesus' traitorous disciple, Judas. For Judas turned Jesus in to the chief priests for thirty

---

[244] Zech. 11:9.
[245] Zech. 11:12-13.

pieces of silver.[246] Later, when Judas saw that Jesus was going to be executed, he was racked with guilt. Therefore, He took the silver back to the chief priests and the elders, but they did not want it. So he threw it into the sanctuary and left to hang himself. The chief priests took the money and bought a plot of land known as the "Potter's Field," which they designated to be used as a cemetery for foreigners.[247] Thus, could it be that Judas is emblematic of the nation as a whole? When Judas realized that Jesus was not going to conquer the Romans and install him as an important lieutenant in the new regime, he sold Jesus out for a pittance. So too, this is how much value the Jewish people as a whole placed on Jesus when He came the first time. Indeed, just as Judas was guilty, so were the Jewish people for giving their assent to Jesus' execution.

Although chapter 11 deals with the subject of the next episode of G-d's judgement upon the Jewish people, this subject is not the emphasis of the book of Zechariah. Rather, the eventual future return from the next exile is the emphasis. This return will be the final return that will take place at the end of history. Following this return, the Jews will be sovereign and they will know peace. Never again will they be threatened by a hostile foreign power. G-d will be in their midst and they will know Him and honor Him. However, there will be a final battle leading up to this new state of reality, and much is written about it in the book of Zechariah. This time when the Gentile armies come and attack Jerusalem, things will turn out differently as the Gentile soldiers will be on the receiving end of the horrors of war. The second example of a shocking verse in Zechariah has to do with this final battle:

---

[246] Mt. 26:14-16.
[247] Mt. 27:3-10.

2. Now this will be the plague with which the
   L-rd will strike all the peoples who have gone
   to war against Jerusalem; their flesh will rot
   while they stand on their feet, and their eyes
   will rot in their sockets, and their tongue will
   rot in their mouth.[248]

Wow! This is the judgement that the enemy combatants will face on the day they rush the gates of Jerusalem. This battle is known to Christians as the battle of Armageddon. It is named after the ancient city of Megiddo which sat upon a hill overlooking a broad plain in the Jezreel valley. It is famous for the ancient battles that took place there.[249] According to the book of Revelation, the armies of the world will converge upon this site at the end of time for one final battle.[250]

What is being predicted in the above startling verse could be the effects of modern weaponry. Perhaps some hideous chemical weapon will cause this horror. It may be that G-d will turn a barrage of missiles back and they will detonate on the people who launched them. Following the collapse of Jerusalem in 70 CE, the Roman army went southeast to remove the enclave of Jews who took shelter on the plateau of Masada. Masada rises a quarter mile above the surrounding terrain. In Masada, a new siege ensued until the Romans built a ramp all the way from the desert floor up to the wall surrounding the encampment. The Roman soldiers constructed a battering ram, moved it into position, and proceeded to pound the stone wall until they knocked a

---

[248] Zech. 14:12.

[249] One of these ancient battles is mentioned in Zechariah 12:11 (which is the verse after the subject verse for this chapter). In that case, the godly king, King Josiah, was slain in the battle that took place at the village of Hadadrimmon (which is located in this plain.)

[250] Rev. 16:13-16.

section of it down. However, the Jews inside quickly built an inner wall made out of wood beams and soil. The new inner wall was softer, and it could absorb the blows of the battering ram. At this point, the Roman commander decided to take a new tact and set fire to the wood. Josephus recorded what happened next:

> . . . so he (the Roman commander, Silva) gave order that the soldiers should throw a great number of burning torches upon it: accordingly, as it was chiefly made of wood, it soon took fire; and when it was once set on fire, its hollowness made the fire spread to a mighty flame. Now, at the very beginning of this fire, a north wind that then blew proved terrible to the Romans; for by bringing the flame downward, it drove it upon them, and they were almost in despair of success, as fearing their machines would be burnt: but after this, on a sudden the wind changed into the south, as if it were done by divine Providence; and blew strongly the contrary way, and carried the flame, and drove it against the wall, which was now on fire through its entire thickness. So the Romans, having now assistance from G-d, returned to their camp with joy, and resolved to attack their enemies the very next day; on which occasion they set their watch more carefully that night, lest any of the Jews should run away from them without being discovered.[251]

---

[251] Josephus, *Wars* 7.8.5 (315-319).

What happened that night on top of the plateau is legendary.[252] But the point is that the Romans and Josephus believed that G-d intervened and caused the wind to change direction, thus sparing the Romans from disaster and ensuring their victory. Did G-d cause the wind to shift directions? Certainly, He did not prevent the wind from aiding the Romans. Perhaps this is another instance where G-d removed His favor from the Jews?

In light of this historic example, could it be that the next time the Roman soldiers assemble outside of Jerusalem and launch their weapons, the wind will again play a factor in the outcome? Only this time, could it be that G-d will protect the Jews by raising a mighty wind to push the missiles backwards so that they crash down on the Romans who launched them?

For certain, G-d will intervene in this battle. In Zechariah, we see G-d operating in different ways to ensure victory for the Jews. For example, we see mass confusion occurring amongst the enemy ranks similar to when Gideon fought against the Midianites.[253] We see G-d give the Jerusalem populace superhuman ability to fight as He did with Samson when he fought against the Philistines.[254] And lastly, we see G-d intervene directly to cause the downfall of the enemy combatants as He did on the day the Egyptian army rushed wildly into the Red Sea and drowned.[255]

There is much prophecy in the book of Zechariah. This chapter does not cover all of it. What has been covered so far

---

[252] Ibid., sections 7.8.6 (320) - 7.9.2 (406). That night, the Jewish families chose to commit mass-suicide rather than suffer rape and deaths that would be more violent in the morning. In all, there were 960 men, women, and children who gave up their lives that night. Two women and five children hid and survived.

[253] Zech. 12:4; 14:13.

[254] Zech. 12:8.

[255] Zech. 14:3-5.

was selected to provide the context for the subject verse of this chapter which is also the third example of a shocking statement made by Zechariah. The verse is Zechariah 12:10:

> 3. "... And I will pour out on the house of David and on the inhabitants of Jerusalem, the Spirit of grace and of supplication, so that they will look on Me whom they have pierced; and they will mourn for Him, as one mourns for an only son, and they will weep bitterly over Him, like the bitter weeping over a first-born."[256]

This event takes place immediately following the final battle. The Jews should be euphoric in this moment as G-d will help them overcome an onslaught by the allied forces of the entire Gentile world! Indeed, G-d will appear. But He will have wounds. It will be Jesus. The Jews will experience the guilt that hit Judas, and they will mourn.

How can this be? It is all so confusing. This person is identified by Zechariah as the long-awaited Messiah who will come at the end of history to rebuild the Temple and who will hold the offices of both king and priest. Zechariah calls him both G-d's servant, harkening back to the mortally wounded servant of Isaiah 53, and the Branch, meaning a descendant of King David.[257] However, near the end of the book, Zechariah also identifies this ruler as G-d by calling Him L-rd and invoking the Shema in regard to Him.[258] Fortunately, one day it will all be clear. For this day will come, and G-d will identify Himself exactly the way Zechariah says, by showing the Jewish people His scars.

---

[256] Zech. 12:10.
[257] Zech. 3:8; 6:12-13.
[258] Zech. 14:9.

This event is reminiscent of a similar occurrence that took place two thousand years ago. Following Jesus' crucifixion, His disciples were in a state of bewilderment and mourning. For they were caught off guard when this happened to Jesus, even though He told them it would happen. But then He resurrected and appeared to them, and their sadness and confusion turned to joy and understanding. However, when He came to where they were staying, Thomas was out. When Thomas came back, Jesus had left. The excited disciples told Thomas the good news, but he did not believe it. It just did not make any earthly sense to him. Here is what happened:

> . . . But he said to them, "Unless I shall see in His hands the imprint of the nails, and put my finger into the place of the nails, and put my hand into His side, I will not believe."
>
> And after eight days again His disciples were inside, and Thomas with them. Jesus came, the doors having been shut, and stood in their midst, and said, "Peace *be* with you." Then He said to Thomas, "Reach here your finger, and see My hands; and reach here your hand, and put it into My side; and be not unbelieving, but believing." Thomas answered and said to Him, "My L-rd and my G-d!" Jesus said to him, "Because you have seen Me, have you believed? Blessed *are* they who did not see, and *yet* believed."[259]

It will be the same at the end of time as Jesus will show His wounds again. Then all the people will believe. Of course, it is harder for Jewish people to believe in Jesus today than it

---

[259] Jn. 20:25-29; it should be noted that this story is where we get the expression "a doubting Thomas," which is still in use today.

was for His disciples. Jesus' disciples loved Him. They saw Him walk on water.[260] But Jews today have not seen Him do any miracles. Furthermore, the Jews have been repulsed by Jesus' followers throughout history, for the church has persecuted, coerced, and even committed atrocities against the Jews. Hence, this message is not only confusing and hard to believe, but it may also carry a moral dilemma. You may feel like you are committing betrayal against your own people if you consider Jesus. Albeit, it must always be remembered that the legions of evil "Christians" who oppressed your ancestors were not acting in accord with Jesus' instructions. But rather, they violated His teaching and grossly misrepresented Him.

So, what about Jewish people today? It is advisable to read the Hebrew Bible with an open mind and to pray to G-d for understanding. G-d is good, He will give you the understanding that you need. In Zechariah chapter 7, Zechariah was warning the Jews of his day not to be like their forefathers who wound up in exile in Babylonia. Regarding the earlier generation, he said:

> ". . . But they refused to pay attention, and turned a stubborn shoulder and stopped their ears from hearing. And they made their hearts *like* flint so that they could not hear the law and the words which the L-rd of hosts had sent by His Spirit through the former prophets; therefore great wrath came from the L-rd of hosts. . . ."[261]

These words still apply today. We all must humble ourselves and approach G-d with listening ears and a soft heart that is open to His will. Yes, G-d has included a measure

---

[260] Mt. 14:22-33.
[261] Zech. 7:11-12.

of ambiguity in some of His prophecies. But He has also straightforwardly revealed quite a bit about the future. Further, He has proven to us that He is faithful and good. Now G-d is asking us to place our trust in Him and obey Him. Those who turn to Him in this way will not be disappointed. A few verses after Zechariah 12:10, it says:

> "In that day a fountain will be opened for the house of David and for the inhabitants of Jerusalem, for sin and for impurity. . . ."[262]

Hence, in Zechariah 12 we have a passage that agrees with the Christian New Testament. Namely, the Messiah's wounds are mentioned in connection with the forgiveness of sins. Thus, when Jesus returns, He will reveal Himself to the Jews and provide them with a fountain. Those who choose to drink from the fountain will have their sins forgiven. For, just as choosing to eat a particular piece of fruit caused Adam and Eve to be sent out of G-d's presence, so too, by taking a drink of this water, Jewish people will be able to enter G-d's presence.

---

[262] Zech. 13:1.

25

PUZZLE PIECES

Returning to our metaphor, puzzle pieces fit together to form the picture on the box lid. Sometimes, the picture is a scenic view. Other times, it is a scene from a Walt Disney movie like Snow White or Peter Pan. Obviously, the more pieces there are, the more difficult it is to put the puzzle together. What if you had a box of pieces from a large puzzle with no lid? That would really be challenging. This is the situation we have with Biblical prophecy.

But we can still get started. We can study the Hebrew Bible, and we can pull all the prophecies out and place them face up on the dining room table. Then we can try to form groups with the goal being to place each prophecy with other ones predicting the same future event or person. The final goal would be to see how the groups fit together to form a unified picture. For in every painting, book, or movie, there is a message that the artist is trying to express. So too, we can expect that G-d has placed a message in the overall picture of Biblical prophecy.

A clue to understanding what is being predicted by a prophecy is history. For although technology has changed our world greatly, we humans have not changed all that much. We are motivated by the same basic desires we have always been. People behave largely the same today as they did in antiquity. Therefore, we can expect prophetic events that still lie in the future to mimic events from the past and to feature people acting in the same ways as they always have.

The wildcard in interpreting prophecy is G-d, for we do not understand Him very well. He is righteous and infinite, and we have a weak grasp on those aspects of His nature. Furthermore, He has given us free will, and He has not intervened very often in history. Therefore, as we read prophecies foretelling acts of selfless love that G-d would perform, we are not sure what to make of them. Perhaps it is best to take them at face value.

The overall picture of Biblical prophecy appears to be a panoramic view of history, starting with predictions of the Babylonian Exile and extending up to events that will take place at the very end of human history. It is a bleak picture in which man is speeding towards a cataclysmic end.[263] But, there is a ray of hope in the picture consisting of G-d implementing a plan to rescue people.

This picture has a number of features, each of which is comprised of multiple prophecies. Hence, the prophecies of the Hebrew Bible can be placed into the following groups:

1. The sin and rebellion of man
2. The judgement of the Jews consisting of their defeat to the Babylonians
3. The return of the Jews from the Babylonian Exile

---

[263] Isa. 24:17-20; Jer. 30:4-11; Dan. 12:1; c.f. Mt. 24.

4. The judgement of individual Gentile nations in ancient times such as Moab and Edom[264]

5. A progression of Gentile empires that would impact Israel

6. The ministry and death of the Messiah

7. Another judgement of the Jews consisting of their defeat to the Romans including the redestruction of Jerusalem and the Temple as well as another exile

8. The reemergence of the Roman Empire under the rulership of an evil man at the end of time

9. A great battle which will be won by the Messiah who will terminate Gentile empires forever at that point[265]

10. A final regathering of the Jewish people[266]

11. The restoration of the land of Israel and nature in general

12. The establishment of a new reality in which Jews and Gentiles who have received atonement will be transformed in their hearts and enter into G-d's presence[267]

We could line up all the prophecies in the Hebrew Bible and place them in these groups. Then we could examine each group by itself as well as in relationship to the other groups. This would give us a good understanding of our predicament and G-d's rescue plan. However, that exercise is well beyond the scope of this book. The subject of this book is the Messiah. Therefore, we will try to fit some key prophecies about this

---

[264] Isa. 15-16; 34.

[265] Ps. 2; c.f. Rev. 19:11 ff.

[266] Isa. 54.

[267] Isa. 35; 49:6; 52:15; Dan. 9:24; c.f. Rev. 21:3.

special individual together to see what G-d says the Messiah would be like and what He would do.

Nonetheless, studying the messianic prophecies is no small task as these prophecies make up a substantial percent of the total amount of prophecy in the Hebrew Bible. Furthermore, this is a difficult task as some of these prophecies contain a measure of ambiguity. G-d wanted to tell us what this special individual would do, and yet to leave some of the future surrounding Him as a surprise. Obviously, G-d had a reason for doing that, which we will discuss in Volume 4.

Christians group the messianic prophecies into two subsets. The first one has to do with the role of the Messiah in fulfilling the requirements of the sacrificial system prescribed in the Mosaic Law. The second subset has to do with the role of the Messiah in defeating the Gentile empire that will be in power at the end of time and establishing a new state of reality. By grouping the messianic prophecies into these two subsets and viewing them as taking place at different times, the pieces start to fit together and the puzzle starts to take shape. For example, here are a couple of contrasting verses about the Messiah from Zechariah chapters 9 and 14:

> "Rejoice greatly, O daughter of Zion! Shout *in triumph*, O daughter of Jerusalem! Behold, your king is coming to you; He is just and endowed with salvation, humble, and mounted on a donkey, even on a colt, the foal of a donkey."[268]

and,

> Then the L-rd will go forth and fight against those nations, as when He fights on a day of

---

[268] Zech. 9:9.

battle. And in that day His feet will stand on the Mount of Olives, which is in front of Jerusalem on the east; and the Mount of Olives will be split in its middle from east to west by a very large valley, so that half of the mountain will move toward the north and the other half toward the south. And you will flee by the valley of My mountains, for the valley of the mountains will reach to Azel; yes, you will flee just as you fled before the earthquake in the days of Uzziah king of Judah. Then the L-rd, my G-d, will come, *and* all the holy ones with Him![269]

Here, we see predictions of two clearly different events. In the second event, the Messiah is G-d, and He touches down on the Mount of Olives along with a retinue of heavenly beings. A mighty earthquake will occur at His feet, and a wide valley will form through which people will flee. A few verses later, Zechariah tells us that He will go on to be the king over the entire earth.[270] In the first passage, the king arrives but no one is fleeing. Rather, the people are shouting in celebration. In this event, the king comes in the exact opposite way, not with a show of great power, but rather with a display of great humility. He approaches the capital seated on a donkey colt.

Of course, the first passage has already come to pass as Jesus approached Jerusalem seated on a donkey colt when He came down the Mount of Olives. It was the culmination of His mission as He would surrender His life as a sacrifice a few days later.

---

[269] Zech. 14:3-5.
[270] Zech. 14:9.

Christians see the passage from Zechariah 14 as the second coming of Christ. He will come back in the last days to put an end to the wickedness of man.[271] Then He will restore love and peace to the earth.

The first coming was necessary in order for the Messiah to be able to restore humanity to a new reality in which people will enter G-d's presence. Without Jesus paying the price for sins, then His second coming could only result in His termination of mankind. For G-d is just, and He will not compromise justice. Therefore, Jesus came two thousand years ago and gave up His life for all who are willing to open their hearts to G-d and receive His forgiveness.

Hence, when prophecy is viewed through the lens of there being two comings of the Messiah, the passages fit together nicely and a lot of things start to make sense. That there is a gap of time between these two events is unclear in prophecies such as Isa. 61:1-3 and Zechariah 9:9-10, which are double-reference prophecies. But it is clear in Daniel 9:26 in which the gap separating the two comings of the Messiah is conspicuous. Further, the gap between the two comings is important, for G-d has been working all this time to execute a new phase in His plan. Namely, He has extended beyond Israel to reach the Gentiles with His offer of forgiveness.

Human sin is one of the main themes of Biblical prophecy. For example, we see this in the book of Isaiah. Isaiah is a long book. It covers all of the prophetic groups listed above, and it starts with a very explicit presentation of the sinfulness of the Jewish people. As the book proceeds, Isaiah also covers the subject of Gentile sin. Indeed, Isaiah spends the first thirty-nine chapters trying to convince us that we are all sinners in

---

[271] Mt. 24.

dire need of a savior. Here is the metaphor from Isaiah chapter 1 describing our spiritual health:

> Alas, sinful nation, people weighed down with iniquity, offspring of evildoers, sons who act corruptly! They have abandoned the L-rd, they have despised the Holy One of Israel, they have turned away from Him.
>
> Where will you be stricken again, as you continue in *your* rebellion? The whole head is sick, and the whole heart is faint. From the sole of the foot even to the head there is nothing sound in it, *only* bruises, welts, and raw wounds, not pressed out or bandaged, nor softened with oil.[272]

The Jews at that time had no idea how thoroughly sinful they were. Isaiah was not excoriating them so much as he was teaching them.

The books of Jeremiah and Daniel agree with the first thirty-nine chapters of Isaiah on how sin is our foundational problem. Most of Jeremiah is about Jewish sin, with the end of the book being about the sin of the Gentiles. Most of Daniel discusses the evil nature of the Gentile empires and the arrogance of their rulers, while chapter 9 covers the subject of Jewish sin. All three of these books prophesy the eventual outcomes for the nation of Israel and the Gentile nations and empires. They also discuss the subjects of Heaven and Hell which are the two possible outcomes for individuals.

In this life, we reap what we sow; we experience the results of our sins. We also sustain injuries caused by the sins of others. Worse still, we are facing a sentence of eternal

---

[272] Isa. 1:4-7.

judgement for our sins. This is our predicament. Thank G-d that He is loving and has come up with a rescue plan to deliver us from our plight. However, G-d is also just and He will not compromise justice. Therefore, there must be an atoning sacrifice. Someone has to pay, and not an animal. Animal sacrifices were never efficacious. They just painted a picture of how desperate our need is. The real sacrifice would have to be a human in order to pay the price for humans. But He would also have to be G-d. For He would have to be without sin in order to be able to pay for the sins of another, and He would have to be infinite to pay the price for the sins of all of us as opposed to only one other human. According to G-d's plan, a Messiah would come who would pay this tremendous cost. This event is the centerpiece of G-d's plan, and that is why a great deal of the prophesy in the Hebrew Bible has to do with this individual and His sacrificial death. Here is a list of the elements of the Messiah's life and death that are predicted in the Hebrew Bible:

1. That He would be born
2. His lineage
3. His character
4. That He would be G-d in human form
5. That He would be killed
6. How He would be killed
7. Why it would be necessary for Him to die
8. That G-d would forsake Him
9. A couple ancillary details that would be unique to His execution
10. The timing of His death
11. His resurrection
12. A great movement that would start following His death and resurrection

Of course, some of these elements appear to be self-contradictory, like for example number four, that the Messiah would be G-d in human form, and number eight, that G-d would forsake Him. Needless to say, we can't just plow ahead without acknowledging this apparent contradiction. As we proceed through this chapter, we will note instances of these two elements as they appear in different prophecies. Then, later in the chapter, we will consider this dilemma.

Now let's examine the prophecies we have covered in this book and see how well they fit together and what the picture is that they form.

Isaiah 53: This passage continues with the subject of our sinfulness from the first half of Isaiah and it foretells G-d's solution to our problem. Namely, a special individual would come and offer up His life as a sacrifice for our sins. Isaiah calls this individual the "Righteous One" and G-d's "Servant." Here are verses 5 through 11:

> . . . But He was pierced through for our transgressions, He was crushed for our iniquities; the chastening for our well-being *fell* upon Him, and by His scourging we are healed. All of us like sheep have gone astray, each of us has turned to his own way; but the L-rd has caused the iniquity of us all to fall on Him.
>
> He was oppressed and He was afflicted, yet He did not open His mouth; like a lamb that is led to slaughter, and like a sheep that is silent before its shearers, so He did not open His mouth. By oppression and judgement He was taken away; and as for His generation, who considered that He was cut

off out of the land of the living, for the transgression of my people to whom the stroke *was due*? His grave was assigned with wicked men, yet He was with a rich man in His death, because He had done no violence, nor was there any deceit in His mouth.

But the L-rd was pleased to crush Him, putting *Him* to grief; if He would render Himself as a guilt offering, He will see *His* offspring, He will prolong *His* days, and the good pleasure of the L-rd will prosper in His hand. As a result of the anguish of His soul, He will see *it* and be satisfied; by His knowledge the Righteous One, My Servant, will justify the many, as He will bear their iniquities.

Here we see that this person would not be like us. He would be sinless. Yet, He would be oppressed and subjected to violence. In verse 5, it tells us that He would be scourged, and His flesh would be pierced. Finally, in verse 8 it says that this special, righteous servant would be "cut off out of the land of the living."

At the end of Isaiah chapter 52, we are given a foreshadowing of the horror this "Righteous One" would face as it says that His appearance would be "marred more than any man, and His form more than the sons of men." He would face the unbearable. In Isaiah 53:3, it says that He would be despised by the nation. A few verses later, it predicts that He would go through this event without opening His mouth. This brave man would not say a word to defend Himself or to attack His enemies.[273] In verse 10, it says that He would "render

---

[273] Mt. 27:11-26; Jn. 19:4-16; and 1 Pet. 2:23-24.

Himself as a guilt offering." In other words, He would voluntarily give up His life for the sake of others. It also says another thing in verse 10, a most amazing thing, that "the L-rd was pleased to crush Him."

An ancillary detail pertaining to His burial is given. Namely, as you would expect, this despised individual would be assigned a grave along with the lowly of Jewish society. But something would happen and He would wind up being buried in the grave of a rich man.[274]

His resurrection is alluded to in the lower portion of chapter 53. For, though His life would be "poured out . . . to death," nonetheless, His days would be "prolonged."[275]

Psalm 22: In this prophecy, King David foretells that he will undergo persecution and suffer a gruesome death. Except, what is forecast never happened to him. The only wounds that are mentioned here are to his hands and feet. But it also describes how this event would be so grueling that he would become dehydrated and exhausted. In addition, his bones would pop out of their sockets and his heart would suffer some form of trauma. This is a description of what happens to a crucifixion victim. Yet, David wrote this psalm four hundred years before crucifixion would be known in Israel. But again, G-d can see the future. He knew that wicked emperors would go on to employ this form of execution in order to coerce occupied peoples to capitulate. Furthermore, He foresaw this particular crucifixion which would be perpetrated against one of David's descendants, the Messiah.

This poor soul would undergo something so hard that He would become disfigured. It appears that Gentiles would

---

[274] Isa. 53:9.
[275] Isa. 53:8-12.

perform the execution as the executioners are pictured as animals. For, in other passages in the Hebrew Bible, G-d likens the Gentiles to predatory animals. This is a fitting metaphor based on the heartless brutality the Romans, Greeks, and others inflicted upon their enemies.[276] Another group of people, presumably the Jews, would watch and mock the victim. In fact, it says that he would be "despised" by the other group of people. This is the same Hebrew word that is used in Isaiah 53:3 which also describes how the Jews would view this person.

Like Isaiah 53, Psalm 22 confirms that death would indeed come to the Messiah. Furthermore, in this psalm we see that this individual would cry out to G-d, but G-d would "forsake Him!"[277] This detail correlates with Isaiah 53:10 in which G-d "crushed" the servant who rendered His life as a guilt offering for the sins of mankind.

An ancillary detail is provided in this prophecy as well. It was unrelated to the practice of crucifixion, yet it was something that G-d could see would take place during the Messiah's crucifixion. G-d included it simply so that we could identify the particular execution and victim that were being predicted in this psalm. Namely, in verses 17 (18) and 18 (19), it is predicted that the Gentiles who would execute Him would also gamble for His clothes.

Finally, in the second half of the psalm it says that this event would lead to people all over the earth turning to G-d and worshipping Him.

Daniel 9: Daniel 9 is quite a chapter. As Daniel studied the scroll of Jeremiah, he read where it was predicted that the Babylonian Exile would last seventy years. Furthermore, he

---

[276] Dan. 7-8.
[277] Ps. 22:1 (2)-5 (6).

realized that the amount of time the Jews had been in exile was getting close to seventy years! Yet, Daniel also knew how sinful the Jewish people were. Therefore, he could not comprehend how G-d could end His judgement of the Jews. So, he prayed. He confessed at length the sins of the Jews including his sins. Then he asked G-d to forgive the Jews and allow them to return to their land and rebuild Jerusalem and the Temple.

Lo and behold, as Daniel prayed, the angel Gabriel came to him and revealed another prophecy, and it also included lengths of time. This prophecy was about the Jewish people, and it laid out their future all the way to the end of time. Indeed, Gabriel let Daniel know that the Jews would return home and rebuild Jerusalem and the Temple. But it says that after a period of 483 years, the Messiah would be cut off. Further, Jerusalem and the Temple would be torn down again, and the Jews would be deported again as well. Then the prophecy predicted an interim period of unspecified length in which the Jews would remain in exile. Finally, Daniel prophesied that G-d will renew His relationship with the Jews and work with them again for the final seven years of history. During this time, a particularly evil man will rise to the top of a revived Roman Empire. In the middle of the seven-year period, he will oppress the Jewish people and perform an abomination in the Temple, which will have been rebuilt by then. However, G-d will have the final say. This man's reign will be terminated, and so will wicked Gentile empires from that point on and forevermore.

Once G-d destroys the final Gentile empire, His rescue plan for humanity will be completed. His plan will accomplish the following six goals: to end this great episode of blasphemy by the Antichrist; to end human sin; to make atonement for sin; to establish a new reality in which humans will be transformed into righteous beings; to fulfill all the prophecies in the Hebrew Bible and reveal the meaning of Biblical prophecy; and to dwell in the Temple and be accessible to everyone.[278]

It should be noted that the Hebrew word for "cut off" which is used in reference to the Messiah in verse 26 is different from the word that is used in Isaiah 53 for the killing of the Servant, but it is a synonym. So, just like Isaiah 53, and just like Psalm 22, we have a prediction of the Messiah being put to death. In this passage, Daniel gives a specific historical marker for when to start the prophetic time clock, and he gives a length of time of 483 years until the death of the Messiah. These details place the Messiah's death in the early 30s CE. Thus, in verses 24 through 27, Daniel connects the killing of the Messiah to the fulfillment of the six goals of G-d's plan for humanity. In fact, the sacrificial death of the Messiah is so central to G-d's plan that Daniel predicted half a millennium in advance the exact time the Messiah would be executed. G-d provided this prophecy so that the Jews could identify the Messiah when His death took place.

Zechariah 12:10: There is quite a bit of prophecy in this book, and much of it has to do with the end of time and the second coming of the Messiah.[279] For example, in Zechariah 12 we read about the final battle in which the armies of the world will encircle Jerusalem and try to tear it down one more time:

> "Behold, I am going to make Jerusalem a cup
> that causes reeling to all the peoples around;
> and when the siege is against Jerusalem, it

---

[278] Dan. 9:24.

[279] There is also prophecy in the Christian New Testament about the second coming of the Messiah, including Mt. 24, Rev. 19, et.al.

will also be against Judah. And it will come about in that day that I will make Jerusalem a heavy stone for all the peoples; all who lift it will be severely injured. And all the nations of the earth will be gathered against it. In that day," declares the L-rd, "I will strike every horse with bewilderment, and his rider with madness. But I will watch over the house of Judah, while I strike every horse of the peoples with blindness. . . ."[280]

The whole world will oppose G-d and His people. Perhaps the Gentiles will remember what happened when the Roman general, Titus, breached the walls and massacred the Jews in Jerusalem in 70 CE. However, apparently they will forget what happened to King Sennacherib of Assyria when he showed up in the early 600s BCE and G-d took the lives of 185,000 Assyrian troops in a single night.[281] So, the heathen soldiers will come again. But it will not be a fair fight and they will all die. For G-d will fight on the side of the Jews. In fact, never again will G-d judge the Jews. From this point on, the Jews will only know G-d's love and acceptance.[282]

Earlier in this chapter, we read another passage from Zechariah about the Messiah's appearance at the end of time. It was from Zechariah 14 in which it is prophesied that the Messiah will land on the Mount of Olives, the earth will quake beneath His feet, and a valley will form. For the Messiah will be G-d.[283] Of course, long before Zechariah wrote this passage,

---

[280] Zech. 12:2-4.
[281] Isa. 37:36.
[282] Isa. 12:1-3; 61:2b-3.
[283] Zech. 14:3-5.

Isaiah clearly stated that the Messiah would be G-d in Isa. 9:6 (5)-7 (6):

> For a child will be born to us, a son will be given to us; and the government will rest on His shoulders; and His name will be called Wonderful Counselor, Mighty G-d, Eternal Father, Prince of Peace. There will be no end to the increase of *His* government or of peace, on the throne of David and over his kingdom, to establish it and to uphold it with justice and righteousness from then on and forevermore. [284]

Therefore, in Isaiah chapter 9 we see that the Messiah will be G-d, but He will also be a human, born of the house of David!

So, the Messiah will come at the end of history to put down the rebellion. But there is still one more detail that is revealed about the Messiah in Zechariah. It is in chapter 12, verse 10, where it says that ". . . they will look on Me whom they have pierced; . . .."

Thus, when the Messiah appears at the end of time, He will have wounds! Indeed, He will have been "pierced." This is not the same Hebrew word that is used in reference to the Righteous Servant in Isaiah 53, but it is a synonym.[285] The fact that G-d will be pierced connects this prophecy in Zechariah 12:10 to the prophecy in Isaiah 53. On the final day of history, there will be a great unveiling, and the wounds suffered by the servant in Isaiah 53 will be seen on the body of none other than G-d Himself when He lands on the Mount of Olives.

---

[284] Isa. 9:6 (5)-7a (6a).
[285] R. Laird Harris et.al. eds., *Theological Wordbook of the Old Testament*, Volume 1, (Chicago: Moody Press, 1980) 288.

The first and second comings of the Messiah are crucially important moments in history in which G-d intervenes to implement His rescue plan for mankind. If the overall picture of Biblical prophecy is a panorama of history that includes these rare interventions by G-d, then Isaiah 53 and Zechariah 12:10 are important prophetic puzzle pieces that connect these two parts of the puzzle together.

The Hebrew Bible juxtaposes a righteous individual against humanity in which we are portrayed as being morally corrupt. Two very different events were predicted in which the righteous individual would intervene in history. One will take place at the end of history. The first event was foretold to take place in the early 30s CE. In the first event, numerous details of the righteous individual's life and death were predicted. These details read like the script of a play that turned out to be Jesus' ministry and crucifixion.

Jesus' First Coming: Indeed, Jesus fulfilled the prophecies of the first coming of the Messiah with a high degree of precision. He was a descendant of David and a legal heir of Solomon. He was kind and gentle to the lowly.[286] He loved His closest friends as well as people He met for the first time, and they loved Him. He did not pursue or acquire any of the rewards of this life.[287] His disciple, Judas, betrayed Him for thirty pieces of silver.[288] Jesus did not defend Himself at His trial.[289] He was executed by crucifixion consisting of the piercing of His hands and feet. The Roman soldiers acted like animals and treated Him inhumanely.[290] The soldiers

---

[286] Isa. 42:1-4; Mt. 8:1-3.
[287] Mt. 8:20.
[288] Mt. 27:1-10.
[289] Mt. 26:59-68; 27:11-14; Jn. 19:8-16.
[290] Mt. 27:27-31; Jn. 19:1-16.

gambled for His tunic. The Jewish onlookers mocked Him. In fact, they spoke the very words and made the very derogatory gestures that Psalm 22 predicted they would.[291] Jesus' death took place in the early 30s CE. He was buried in the tomb of a rich man. Pontius Pilate installed a Roman military detail to guard the tomb. Yet, His body went missing. His disciples claimed that He rose from the dead and appeared to them on multiple occasions. The early opponents of this new branch of Judaism tried to coerce the disciples to recant their testimonies. For, Jesus' enemies could not disprove Jesus' resurrection as His body was gone. But alas, Jesus' disciples went to their deaths rather than recant. In the following years, this new form of Judaism spread like wildfire to the Gentiles in Europe, Asia, and Africa. Christianity continues to spread still today as missionaries are taking Jesus' offer of forgiveness to the remotest pockets of civilization on earth.

Here is a passage from the Gospel of Luke about an interaction Jesus had which is representative of His dealings with Jewish people in general:

> Now one of the Pharisees was requesting Him to dine with him. And He entered the Pharisee's house, and reclined *at the table*. And behold, there was a woman in the city who was a sinner; and when she learned that He was reclining *at the table* in the Pharisee's house, she brought an alabaster vial of perfume, and standing behind *Him* at His feet, weeping, she began to wet His feet with her tears, and kept wiping them with the hair of her head, and kissing His feet, and anointing them with the perfume. Now when

---

[291] Mt. 27:39-44; Lk. 23:35.

the Pharisee who had invited Him saw this, he said to himself, "If this man were a prophet He would know who and what sort of person this woman is who is touching Him, that she is a sinner." And Jesus answered and said to him, "Simon, I have something to say to you." And he replied, "Say it, Teacher." "A certain moneylender had two debtors: one owed five hundred denarii, and the other fifty. When they were unable to repay, he graciously forgave them both. Which of them therefore will love him more?" Simon answered and said, "I suppose the one whom he forgave more." And He said to him, "You have judged correctly." And tuning toward the woman, He said to Simon, "Do you see this woman? I entered your house; you gave Me no water for My feet, but she has wet My feet with her tears, and wiped them with her hair. You did not anoint My head with oil, but she anointed My feet with perfume. For this reason I say to you, her sins, which are many, have been forgiven, for she loved much; but he who is forgiven little, loves little." And He said to her, "Your sins have been forgiven." And those who were reclining *at the table* with Him began to say to themselves, "Who is this man who even forgives sins?" And He said to the woman, "Your faith has saved you; go in peace."[292]

---

[292] Lk. 7:36-50.

This is quite a story. This sinful woman, likely a prostitute, crashed a party at the home of a religious person and made a scene. She was weeping; her tears fell on Jesus' feet, and she kissed His feet and anointed them with perfume. The guests witnessed this spectacle, and then continued to smell her perfume on Jesus' feet for quite some time. What is even more shocking is that Jesus did not try to stop her, but rather, He received this outpouring of love. Then, of all things, He told her that her sins were forgiven! The pharisee who invited Jesus to his home was confused. He had heard that Jesus was a rabbi and perhaps a prophet. But upon watching this interaction between Jesus and this sinful woman, he did not know what to think of Jesus. For, he believed that G-d is opposed to the sinful. Therefore, how could Jesus be so warm and receptive towards her? Jesus tried to explain to him that all have sinned and need forgiveness, albeit some more than others, like this woman. She understood her desperate need for forgiveness from G-d. Hence, when Jesus showed her acceptance, she was overcome with emotion. This story is a microcosm of Jesus' mission. He came to provide forgiveness and extend a warm offer of salvation to all people.[293]

In the days following this interaction, Jesus' message of radical forgiveness was not well received by the Jewish religious leaders. In addition, He made bold claims about His identity which offended them.[294] Furthermore, He conflicted with the religious leaders over their traditions. Jesus knew that His conflict with them would lead to His death. In fact, He told His disciples on multiple occasions that He was going to be killed.[295] When the time drew near for Jesus to be crucified, He was distraught. Jesus knew all too well the

---

[293] Jn. 3:16-17; Rev. 3:20.
[294] e.g. Jn. 8:53-59.
[295] e.g. Mt. 16:21.

prophecies of His death, and He understood how awful it would be. Then He said to His disciples,

> "My soul is deeply grieved, to the point of death; remain here and keep watch with Me." And He went a little beyond *them*, and fell on His face and prayed, saying, "My Father, if it is possible, let this cup pass from Me; yet not as I will, but as Thou wilt."[296]

The answer was no. The only way for any human being to go to heaven is to receive atonement for their sins.[297] G-d will not compromise justice. Therefore, the price of atonement had to be paid. For that purpose, Jesus came.[298] Following His prayer, Jesus knew the answer, and He stepped forward to bear this grim burden.

Jesus' Second Coming: There is a good amount of prophecy in the Christian New Testament, and almost all of it refers to the end of time. It meshes with the prophecy in the Hebrew Bible, and it adds new details. Of course, the book of Revelation is well known, albeit it is not well understood. The Greek word for revelation is apokalypsis which refers to something that has been uncovered or revealed. This is where the English word apocalypse comes from. Today this term has come to be associated with the content of the book of Revelation. Namely, it is associated with the cataclysmic end of history in which the evil Gentile world rulers will wreak havoc on the world. However, the Greek word itself simply means to reveal something that is unknown. John uses the word apokalypsis in the first verse of Revelation. This verse is

---

[296] Mt. 26:38-39.

[297] Jn.14:6; 1 Pet. 2:24; 3:18.

[298] Mt. 20:28.

somewhat paradoxical. For, it speaks of revealing the future, but the writing style in Revelation is highly symbolic and difficult to understand.

Jesus' disciple John wrote the book of Revelation in the 90s CE. He was shown visions of the end of time, but he had to draw on things from his world to try to describe what he was seeing. What if John received a vision of World War I? It would have been very hard for him to describe that war. War in John's day consisted of two battle lines facing each other in which the soldiers wielded swords, spears, shields, and courage. The commander who felt he had the advantage would charge the other side. In fact, this method of conducting battle persisted for over three thousand years, from the time of David all the way up to the start of World War I.[299] During this very long time span, the major development in warfare was simply the replacement of spears with rifles. World War I started with this same method of conducting battle, but then everything changed in the blink of an eye. The widespread employment of machine guns quickly forced the two sides to dig trenches in which to protect their lines of soldiers. Imagine if John had been shown scenes from World War I. How would he describe machine guns, artillery, flamethrowers, barbed wire, tanks, poison gas, and gas masks? Of course, within a few decades, military weaponry took another quantum leap forward as aircraft carriers, incendiary bombs, Higgins boats, submarines, death camps, and the atom bomb were developed for use in World War II. Needless to say, technology has continued to move forward since the end of World War II. Poor John saw weapons wreaking havoc on man and nature from the very end of time, things that even we have not seen yet. Hence, he used terms such as burning torches falling from the sky and poisoning

---

[299] 1 Sam. 17:1-21.

rivers.[300] This sounds like a missile attack in which the missiles are carrying chemical weapons in an attempt to take out the enemy's water supply. In this case, John reports that the attack will succeed as a third of the world's water supply will be poisoned. But the point is that John was severely limited in his ability to describe what he saw. So too, people who lived before the modern age had no basis upon which to understand his predictions. Today, not completely, but substantially, we can understand what he was predicting!

Essentially, Revelation chapters 4 through 19 are a lengthy elaboration of Daniel 9:27. In the first three chapters of Revelation, Jesus gave John some instructions to pass on to seven specific Christian churches in Asia Minor.[301] But after chapter three, although Jesus is mentioned, Christian churches are not. Rather, the Jews are the subject. For, just as Daniel predicted in verse 27, G-d will return to work with the Jewish people for the final phase of history. Also, two periods of three and a half years are used as the basis for the timeline of events in the book of Revelation.[302] These periods correspond to the two halves of the seven-year period that are described in Daniel 9:27. In addition, there is a whole chapter in Revelation dealing with the evil ruler of the future world Empire.[303] In Daniel 9:26, he is called "the prince who is to come"; in Revelation, he is called "the beast."[304]

One of the six goals of G-d listed in Daniel 9:24 was fulfilled by Jesus at His first coming, "to make atonement for iniquity." The other five will be fulfilled upon Jesus' return. Among others, these goals include: "to finish the

---

[300] Rev. 8:10.

[301] Rev. 1:11.

[302] Rev. 11:1-3; 12:1-17; et.al.

[303] Rev. 13.

[304] Rev. 13:4.

transgression," "to make and end of sin," and "to bring in everlasting righteousness." In Revelation chapter 19, John records the final moment in heaven before Jesus departs to return to earth and accomplish these goals:

> And I saw heaven opened; and behold, a white horse, and He who sat upon it is called Faithful and True; and in righteousness He judges and wages war. And His eyes *are* a flame of fire, and upon His head are many diadems; and He has a name written *upon Him* which no one knows except Himself. And *He* is clothed with a robe dipped in blood; and His name is called the Word of G-d. And the armies which are in heaven, clothed in fine linen, white and clean, were following Him on white horses. And from His mouth comes a sharp sword, so that with it He may smite the nations; and He will rule them with a rod of iron; and He treads the wine press of the fierce wrath of G-d, the Almighty. And on His robe and on His thigh He has a name written, "KING OF KINGS, AND L-RD OF L-RDS."[305]

When He returns, Jesus will end the reigns of the Antichrist and all the other sinful Gentile world rulers. The "transgression" mentioned by Daniel refers to the abomination committed by the Antichrist in the Temple.[306] Yet, it will, not just be the Antichrist, but rather, society as a whole will be godless. Hate will grow strong, and love will

---

[305] Rev. 19:11-16.
[306] 2 Thes. 2:3-4.

shrivel.[307] Life will be cheap, and a tremendous number of people will die in the coming world war. Atrocities will likely be brought back. Rightly will Jesus come back and end human history. At the moment of His return, all the Gentile armies will be gathered in Israel.[308] Following their defeat, eternity will begin in which G-d will transform the hearts of those who have received atonement for their sins.[309] Mercifully, He will take away our sin and cleanse us so that we are righteous. Here is a peek into this new state of reality:

> And I saw a new heaven and a new earth; for the first heaven and the first earth passed away, and there is no longer *any* sea. And I saw the holy city, new Jerusalem, coming down out of heaven from G-d, made ready as a bride adorned for her husband. And I heard a loud voice from the throne, saying, "Behold, the tabernacle of G-d is among men, and He shall dwell among them, and they shall be His people, and G-d Himself shall be among them, and He shall wipe every tear from their eyes; and there shall no longer be *any* death; there shall no longer be *any* mourning, or crying, or pain; the first things have passed away." And He who sits on the throne said, "Behold, I am making all things new." And He said, "Write, for these words are faithful and true." And he said to me, "It is done. I am the Alpha and the Omega, the beginning and the

[307] 2 Tim. 3:1-5.
[308] Rev. 14:17-20; 16:12-16.
[309] Jer. 31:31-33.

end. I will give to the one who thirsts from the
spring of the water of life without cost. . . ."[310]

This is the culmination of G-d's plan in which we will be
returned to the state Adam and Eve gave up. We will be with
G-d! He repeats this twice as it is so fantastic that our first
inclination is to think that He is speaking figuratively. In
eternity, life will not be characterized by disappointment and
pain. Rather, we will be free from guilt, and we will experience
joy as we give and receive pure love in our relationships with
G-d and other people. Thus, He speaks of giving us water from
the "spring of the water of life" to quench our deepest needs.
The speaker of this statement identifies Himself as the "Alpha
and the Omega." This is Jesus who is also identified in this
way later in the book of Revelation.[311] Jesus can provide the
water without cost as He already paid the price of salvation for
the whole world when He came to earth the first time.[312] Who
are those who will be granted to drink of this water? These
people are the ones who "thirst." They place greater value on
going to heaven than the rewards of this life.[313] They fear
winding up in hell, the possibility of which is mentioned in
multiple places in Revelation.[314] Therefore, they turn to G-d
and ask Him to show them His pathway.

* * * * *

In conclusion, if you try to group like prophecies together, and
if you try to connect the different groups of prophecies, then
the message G-d embedded in prophecy begins to emerge. It
is a message of a problem and a solution. For we have a

---

[310] Rev. 21:1-6.
[311] Rev. 22:12-21; c.f. Isa. 55; Jn. 4:1-42; Rev. 7:9-17.
[312] Mt. 28:18-20.; 1 Pet. 2:21-25; 3:18; 1 Jn. 2:2.
[313] Mt. 6:19-34; Heb. 11:1-16.
[314] Rev. 20:15; 21:8.

problem, and it is us. We have sinned and caused great destruction both as a race and as individuals. G-d's solution is to send a savior. The prophecies of G-d's savior fit into two groups. One group predicted a savior who would come and die as a sacrifice to set us free as individuals from having to pay the price of justice for our sins. The prophecies in Isaiah 53, Psalm 22, Daniel 9, et.al. make up this group. These prophecies contain similar details which connect them together. They also contain unique details which combine to form a complete picture of the Messiah's ministry and execution. The fact that there are multiple prophecies predicting the execution of the Messiah coupled with the gripping writing in these prophecies indicates the importance of His death in G-d's plan. The other group of prophecies predicts a savior who will come to put an end to the wicked rulers and governments of man that start wars and steal people's basic human rights. Each of our lives is a gift from G-d, but a select group of powerful men down through the ages have arrogated to themselves control over other people's lives. One day, G-d will say, "No more." The prophecies in this group include Isaiah 9, Daniel 9, Zechariah 12 and 14, et.al.

G-d has provided us with a rich assortment of messianic prophecies in the Hebrew Bible. We should read these prophecies and consider them. Why is it predicted that the Messiah would be killed in the early 30s of the first century CE? Why will almighty G-d come to earth at the end of time and have wounds? Jesus being crucified to pay the price for the sins of mankind answers these questions well.

And yet, most Jewish people do not believe that Jesus is the Messiah. If you agree with the commonly held Jewish position that Jesus was only a man and the prophecies in the Hebrew Bible are not about Him, then how do you interpret these prophecies? Surely G-d's prophecies are not haphazard. Rather, they fit together to form a cohesive whole. Apart from

Jesus, how do you harmonize the two contrasting sets of prophecies about the Messiah? Thus far, the interpretations that have come from Jewish scholars have not been very strong. For example, Rabbi Singer has written a lengthy interpretation of Isaiah 53.[315] Simply put, his explanation is that since Isaiah calls the Jews G-d's servant in other passages, then the subject of chapter 53 must be the Jews because Isaiah uses the term G-d's servant in 52:13 and 53:11. Thus, Rabbi Singer sees Isaiah chapter 53 as a presentation of the suffering of the Jewish people down through the ages. Surely the Jews have suffered tremendously throughout history. But this passage cannot be about the Jews, for never is it asserted in the Hebrew Bible that they suffered to pay the price for the sins of others. Rather, the Hebrew Bible is emphatic that their suffering has always been due to their sins. Furthermore, Isaiah goes out of his way in chapter 53 to delineate this servant as someone other than the Jewish people.

Of course, interpreting the prophecy in the Hebrew Bible as predicting two comings of the Messiah and identifying Jesus as the Messiah still does not answer every question.

Rightly do Jews ask how G-d can be one and yet be three as Christians say. After all, as it says in the Shema, "Hear, O Israel! The L-rd is our G-d, the L-rd is One!"[316]

The Bible answers the questions that we need to know the most. Namely, the Bible tells us what G-d's character is like, who we are, how we got where we are today, and how we can be delivered from our sins. The Bible is clear on all of these subjects. Yet, there are other questions that are only broached lightly in the Bible. An example would be the question that was raised earlier in the chapter. Namely, how can the

---

[315] Rabbi Singer 1:91-129.
[316] Deut. 6:4.

Messiah be G-d and yet also be rejected by G-d? Christianity's answer to this question is the doctrine of the trinity. The concept of how G-d can be one and yet also be three is not fully explained in the Hebrew Bible, but some partial answers are provided. For example, in Genesis chapter 1, G-d is presented as having a plural essence:

> Then G-d said, "Let us make man in Our image, according to Our likeness; and let them rule over the fish of the sea and over the birds of the sky and over the cattle and over all the earth, and over every creeping thing that creeps on the earth." And G-d created man in His own image, in the image of G-d He created him; male and female He created them.[317]

Here G-d is speaking in the first person plural and He does it three times. Then He speaks of creating man in His image such that there would be two kinds of people: men and women. Later, in Genesis 2, it says:

> For this cause a man shall leave his father and his mother, and shall cleave to his wife; and they shall become one flesh.[318]

Here, we see the moment when G-d first gave man the gift of marriage. G-d's design is for two people to be so in love and so united that they now see themselves differently than they did before. They both have a new identity. Now they see themselves as parts of a couple and no longer as individuals.

Therefore, could it be with G-d that He is one united entity, and yet comprised of three parts or persons: the

---

[317] Gen. 1:26-27.
[318] Gen. 2:24.

Father, the Son, and the Holy Spirit? So, the answer to the earlier question is that the Messiah is G-d the Son who bears the wrath of G-d the Father in order to pay the price of justice for human beings.

This explanation does not answer every question. But perhaps it is all we need to know right now. In fact, there appears to be a reason why G-d is withholding some information and not answering all of our questions at the present time.

In the book of Jeremiah it says, "In the latter days you will understand this."[319] Jeremiah was aware that we are spiritually confused. Until the end of time comes and everything takes place as the Hebrew Bible says it will, we will not fully understand. But on the last day, there will be an unveiling. G-d will show us His wounds. In an instant, we will all see who G-d is. Furthermore, we will understand what He has been doing throughout history, and we will know beyond a shadow of a doubt that He is truthful, patient, just, and merciful.

Some of the messianic prophecies in the Hebrew Bible are straightforward and clear, but not all of them. Why are some of the prophecies unclear? Why does there need to be an unveiling in which we are caught off guard by the truth? Perhaps it is because accusations have been made against G-d that cause us to be confused about His goodness. But on the last day of history, His innocence will be undeniable. Maybe it has to be this way in order for G-d to restore peace and harmony in the universe. He cannot just proclaim His innocence. It has to be proven. Otherwise, the lies told by the forces of evil will still have life and be able to cause confusion and disorder.

---

[319] Jer. 30:24.

As John the Baptist lay in jail with his life on the line, he became very depressed. He had devoted his life to the will of G-d, and now his fate was up to the whims of a sinful ruler, Herod the tetrarch. John knew the Hebrew Bible well, and he knew that the Messiah would crush the Gentile kingdoms and ascend to the throne of David. Therefore, John wondered why this was happening to him. So, he sent his disciples to ask Jesus if He was indeed the Messiah. Jesus sent them back and had them tell John of His healing ministry and the message of good news He was proclaiming to the poor.[320] Jesus' reply was sufficient for John because he knew that those acts were also parts of the Messiah's mission. So, even though John did not understand why Jesus wasn't overthrowing the Romans and taking control of the government at that time, he was at peace. For John understood that G-d's ways are higher than our ways and G-d has a different timing than we do.

What do you think - are the prophecies Jesus has already fulfilled sufficient for you to believe that He is the Messiah?

---

[320] Mt. 11:1-5.

TO BE CONTINUED. . .

INDEX

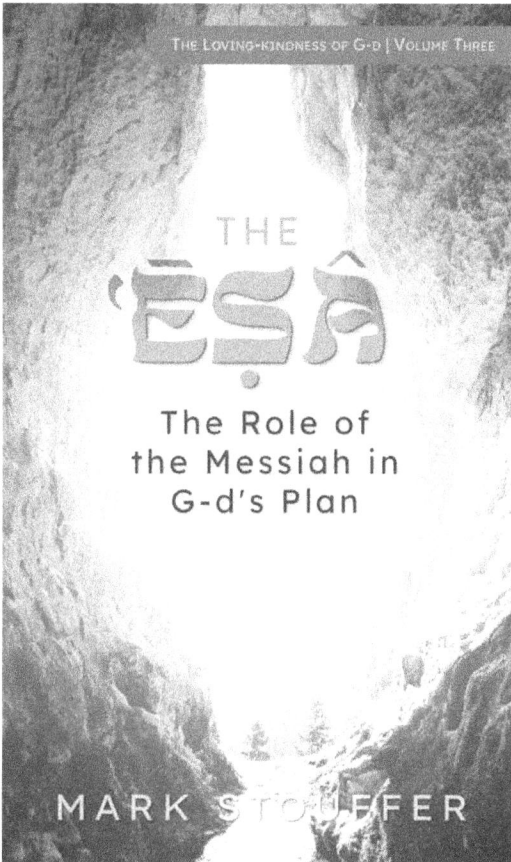

THE LOVING-KINDNESS OF G-D | VOLUME THREE

THE
‘ĒṢÂ

The Role of
the Messiah in
G-d's Plan

MARK STOUFFER

Thank you for reading my book!

If you would like a free, autographed
preview chapter from *The 'Ēṣâ*, go to:

https://lovingkindnessofadonai.com

www.ingramcontent.com/pod-product-compliance
Lightning Source LLC
Chambersburg PA
CBHW051825090426
42736CB00011B/1649